The Nursing Home Crunch

**A Legal and Financial Guide
To Surviving a Long-Term
Nursing Home Stay Without
Losing Your Life Savings**

Edward D. Beasley, JD, LLM
David H. Ferber, JD

Library of Congress Control No: 2003090232
ISBN 1-889902-19-5

Printed in the United States of America
Design by John Hiebert

Published by Beasley & Ferber, PA
                Concord, New Hampshire
Produced by Partnership Book Service
                Hillsboro, Kansas

For additional copies, send $24.95 plus $3.00 shipping and handling per book to
                Beasley & Ferber, PA
                55 Hall Street
                Concord, NH 03301
                (603) 225-5010

Dedication

In memory of my parents, a loving mother who championed the cause of the disadvantaged and a devoted father who is currently fighting a losing battle with Alzheimer's.

Edward D. Beasley

Caretaker spouses of elderly dementia patients toil from dawn to dusk without weekends or holidays. They seek neither reward nor recognition, but simply want the best for their loved one. It is to these courageous people that I dedicate this book.

David H. Ferber

Table of Contents

About the Authors:

Edward D. Beasley, JD, LLM: Attorney Beasley is the founder of Beasley & Ferber, P.A., an Estate Planning and Elder Law Firm with offices in Concord, Bedford, Nashua and Portsmouth, New Hampshire and North Andover, Massachusetts. He received his Bachelor's Degree, Summa Cum Laude, Phi Beta Kappa, from Dartmouth College (1974), his Juris Doctor Degree, Cum Laude, from Washington & Lee University (1978) and his LLM Degree in Taxation from Boston University (1982).

Mr. Beasley has written and published numerous articles on Estate Planning and Elder law including "Trusts for the Average Person," "The Nursing Home Crunch," and "The Ethics of Medicaid Planning." He has appeared as a featured guest on NBC's National Nightly News with Tom Brokaw in a segment entitled "Inheritance Disputes." Attorney Beasley was also featured in a USA TODAY cover story entitled: "Fighting Over the Care of Aging Parents." He is co-author of the book, "Alzheimer's Disease: Fighting for Financial Survival." He lectures frequently on the topic of Elder Law and the legal steps available to protect the life savings of people in nursing homes.

Mr. Beasley is former Chair of the Elder Law Committee of the American Bar Association (General Practice, Solo and Small Firm Section). He is also a member of the

National Academy of Elder Law Attorneys. Mr. Beasley is recognized nationally as an expert in the field of Elder Law, Medicaid and Nursing Home Planning, and Asset Preservation techniques for those afflicted with dementia in general and the dementing illnesses known as Alzheimer's Disease, Huntington's Disease and Amyothrophic Lateral Sclerosis (Lou Gehrig's Disease), in particular.

David H. Ferber, JD: Attorney Ferber is a partner with Beasley & Ferber, P.A. He received his Bachelor's Degree in Psychology, Magna Cum Laude, Phi Beta Kappa, from Columbia University (1981) and his Juris Doctor Degree from Columbia University Law School (1984), where he was a member of the Columbia Human Rights Law Review.

Mr. Ferber is a nationally-published author of articles on Estate and Medicaid Planning, including articles on Charitable Remainder Trusts, The Use of Annuities in Medicaid Planning, The Use of Disclaimers in Estate Planning, Qualified Personal Residence Trusts and the Joint Revocable Trust as a Tool for Estate and Medicaid Planning, among others. He is also the author of articles on Estate Planning for the *Concord Monitor*, Concord, New Hampshire, and the *Laconia Citizen*, Laconia, New Hampshire. He is co-author of the book, "Alzheimer's Disease: Fighting for Financial Survival." He is a frequent lecturer on Estate and Medicaid Planning.

Mr. Ferber is former Vice Chair and Newsletter Editor of the Elder Law Committee of the American Bar Association (General Practice, Solo and Small Firm Section), and is a member of the National Academy of Elder Law Attorneys and of the Elder Law section of the New Hampshire Bar Association. He is a former member of the board of directors of the New Hampshire Family Support Partnerships, and is a former board member of the New Hampshire Coalition Against Elder Abuse, a former Commissioner of the Laconia, New Hampshire, Conservation Commission and a former board member of the Stamford, Connecticut, Shelter for the Homeless. He is a member of the bars of New Hampshire, Massachusetts, Maine and Connecticut.

Introduction

"Last scene of all.

That ends this strange eventful history,
Is second childishness and mere oblivion,

Sans teeth, sans eyes, sans taste, sans everything."

William Shakespeare
"As You Like It"
Act I, Scene vii

It is indisputable that William Shakespeare wrote more works on the "human condition" than any other poet before or since him. His keen sense of all things affecting humanity is reflected in his sonnets, poems, comedies, tragedies and other works. Regrettably, many of us, including today's senior citizens, will face a regression into a "second childishness" and "mere oblivion" prior to death. Despite the miracles of modern medicine, our elderly citizens today are still confronting the loss of teeth, eyes and taste as quoted above by Shakespeare. Many senior citizens spend those final years as residents of nursing homes, where, in addition to the loss of physical abilities and faculties, they end up, as Shakespeare said, "sans everything," having been forced to liquidate all their life savings (their CDs, stocks, bonds, IRAs), including their home to pay for their nursing home care.

Although Shakespeare was no prophet, it was almost as though 400 years ago he could have seen clearly the state of nursing home care and finances in our present time. As many hard working husbands and wives, fathers and mothers, soon discover, if their loved one is forced to obtain care in a nursing home or other long-term care facility, they will be forced into poverty before the government steps in to provide a "safety net." Medicaid, the government program which provides long-term care relief to American citizens, does so only after the family has been essentially wiped out. This book will explain the Medicaid rules and regulations but as most folks know, our system is not designed to pay for the long-term care of our citizens until they have been forced to spend down virtually all of their assets. Simply put, Medicare, the program designed to assist in the medical/health needs of our elderly citizens is not designed, nor ever was designed, to pay for long-term nursing home care. "Spend down" or private payment from one's own private funds is required before Medicaid steps in to pay for long-term care.

In our first book, "Alzheimer's Disease: Fighting for Financial Survival," we detailed many of the same issues we will discuss here. In particular, we discussed how it has been said that the Medicaid rules and regulations are intentionally made vague and almost indecipherable, even by a majority of lawyers (even some who concentrate their practice in Estate Planning), so the layperson, in his time of greatest need, is resigned to the "stacked deck" of the vast bureaucracy known as our government; in addition, it has been reported that a large majority of nursing homes not only fail to inform residents of their legal rights, but often mislead patients and their families in this area.

Thankfully, the reviews on our first book were quite generous. A review published by the "American Journal of Alzheimer's Disease and Other Dementias" in its March-April 2001 issue stated that our book was "an easy-to-understand survey for laypersons on the many legal and financial topics about which Alzheimer's patients, their families and those who work with them should be familiar." The review further states, "Alzheimer's Disease: Fighting for Financial Survival" is rich with resource referrals." Finally, the review stated how we (Beasley and Ferber) feel that no book can be a substitute for an expert lawyer in this area of asset protection and nursing home planning; however, it concluded as follows, "A person who reads this book will be an educated consumer of legal services and will be well prepared to work with an attorney to structure a plan to meet the indicvidual needs of his or her family."

The one minor criticism we received almost universally was that too many folks thought our book only covered planning for those afflicted with Alzheimer's Disease. In writing the book, we specifically chose Alzheimer's Disease due to its high recognition amongst health care providers and the public. We never intended the book to exclude folks recovering from debilitating strokes, heart disease, Lou Gerhig's Disease, multiple sclerosis, Parkinson's Disease, or any other debilitating condition that could render one incapable of caring for himself, and thus subject to nursing home care.

As with our first book, this book is intended as an informative, easy-to-read reference guide for laypersons. It is not intended to be an indictment of our government's failure to assist the elderly and infirm, nor a condemnation of all nursing homes. It is intended to bring some light to an area of much confusion and contradiction. It is our intent to help "level the playing field" between the vast bureaucracy of the Medicaid program, with its massive rules, regulations and technicalities, and the layperson, not schooled in law and facing a time of family crisis. By necessity, there will be some duplication in the information contained herein with what is contained in our first book, particularly as it pertains to the law. This is inevitable, inasmuch as the basic laws and regulations pertaining to Medicaid have changed little or not at all since our last book was published. In addition, any repetition in this book and the last one is probably good, inasmuch as we have found that it is only through repetition that non-lawyers and even many lawyers, come to truly understand this complex area of law.

As with our first book, this book contains a wealth of knowledge in the appendices; some of these appendices contain information needed on a day-by-day basis by families of a loved one facing nursing home care, while others are more complex, delving into the federal laws and how such federal laws contain the rights of all nursing home residents, quality of nursing home life and the adequacy of nursing home care—all guaranteed under existing federal law.

Finally, some may question the "need" for a book discussing the mechanics of the Medicaid system and the legal planning available to avoid complete economic devastation in the event of a prolonged nursing home stay. Perhaps as short a time as 10 years ago there would not have been such a need; however, since the late 1980s there have been a series of law changes which have restricted the rights of citizens to plan effectively to protect their assets from a prolonged nursing home stay. In addition, it was not long ago that a nursing home stay was less than fifty thousand dollars ($50,000) a year; during that same time frame the stock market was booming and Certificates of Deposit were yielding in the double digits. It was quite common then to construct a medicaid/nursing home plan which provided for private pay while still protecting the principal of the assets for the children or spouse of the nursing home resident. After all, if the family had liquid assets of $300,000 plus combined income of social security and pensions of $2,000 per month, the family could "private pay" for the nursing home resident without the urgency with which we are faced now. Interest rates are at unprecedented lows; the stock market has struggled through a downward spiral rivaling the worst on record. Yet, nursing home costs are spiraling through the roof. In even the relatively rural areas of New Hampshire and Massachussetts, we are finding nursing home rates consistently over $70,000 per year; in fact, it is becoming quite common to discover homes where the annual rate is nearing $100,000 per year. In this context, it is obvious why this book is necessary for proper planning. How many families in retirement can withstand the outflow of $100,000 per year should they or their spouse enter a nursing home? (Even if it were for less than the national average stay of approximately two years?) How long could their combined life savings last if they both needed nursing home care? This is elementary. Everyone wants to pay his fair share, and we are big believers in long-term care insurance to pay nursing home bills, but how many families can afford those hefty premiums? If a husband and wife have comfortably retired with $300,000 and their home and one spouse needs nursing home care for only a year, then dies or returns home, what is the "new" standard of living after having paid out approximately $70,000 of their life savings for the care of the nursing home confined spouse? In the nursing home-Medicaid planning context, we are finding that even "wealthy" folks are not wealthy should they or their spouse or both need nursing home care. This is truly not just a "nursing home crunch" but a nursing home "crisis." Many criticize what Elder Law Attorneys such as we do; they view it as exploiting loopholes. Our goal, both in our practice and in writing this book, is not to help wealthy folks evade all responsibility for their long-term care, but provide a plan which has a balanced approach to the problem—one where the client and the society share in the cost of the client's care. It has been, and remains, our law firm's philosophy that no one should be forced to lose everything should they be forced into the need for long-term nursing home care.

Chapter 1:

Useful Nursing Home Information

E very person knows that statistics can be manipulated to make almost any point, pro or con, that the one using the statistics wishes to argue. However, when planning our legal work for our clients, especially long-term planning where a nursing home stay is not imminent but probable, we can draw on statistics to see trends to ensure the client makes the best, informed decision concerning their medical and legal care.

Studies have shown that approximately three out of every five Americans over the age of 65 will need some type of long-term care. The most severely disabled of these citizens (unable to perform three or more activities of daily living) make up approximately five million of our citizenry.

There are currently an approximate 17,000 nursing homes in the country, with a combined resident count of approximately 1.5 million. The actuaries calculate that by the year 2030, there will be five million nursing home patients.

Nearly all nursing homes have some form of certification enabling them to receive Medicaid and Medicare.

Approximately three-quarters of all nursing homes representing four-fifths of all nursing home beds are certified by Medicare and Medicaid. The nursing home bed-occupancy rate, which may vary from region to region, is approximately 90%. The average stay in a nursing home is calculated at approximately two years.

These statistics can be used or abused in any way. The fact is, however, that the odds are great that any senior citizen, male or female, will spend some time in a nursing home. It is not really relevant or of importance to our male clients that they are unique because the largest group of seniors in nursing homes are women. Nor does it comfort a family to hear that the average stay in the nursing home may be approximately two years. What is relevant to the family, and the only thing relevant to that family, is that their loved one, husband, wife or parent, is in the nursing home and Medicare will only cover a tiny part of the care and for a very small amount of time. What is relevant to that family is the stark reality that without some planning, all of the family assets can be wiped out if the stay is prolonged for any length of time.

Regrettably, at this point we are in the stage of crisis planning (set forth later in the book) as opposed to advanced planning (also set forth later in the book); the good news is that even at this late stage (nursing home confinement), virtually all of the assets of a married couple may be saved for the single spouse and about 50% of single parent's assets may be saved for their children. This can be done despite the commonly-held belief that nothing can be done in the way of protecting assets unless done three years or five years in advance. Nothing could be further from the truth, as we routinely set up plans for folks already in a nursing home which save all of a clients assets for a healthy spouse or 50% of the assets of a single parent for their children, while still getting our clients approved for Medicaid assistance.

Chapter 2:

What is Medicaid Planning

We remember back to the 1980s when Elder Law was so irrelevant that the American Bar Association did not even have an Elder Law Committee. In fact, Elder Law came under the heading of "Estate Planning." Most estate planning lawyers, even many who practiced Elder Law, did not look at the Medicaid aspect of the client's legal affairs. Underneath the umbrella of Elder Law is the further area of concentration called "Medicaid Planning." Today, with the prohibitive expense of nursing homes, almost all families and virtually all estate planning attorneys pay some heed to the concern of what devastating consequences might befall their clients in the event of a prolonged nursing home stay. In fact, many clients would have no need of true "Estate Planning" in the event they encountered a prolonged nursing home stay inasmuch as the nursing home stay would or could deplete the entire estate of all but the wealthy.

Many laypersons think that manipulating legal techniques to essentially make wealthy folks Medicaid eligible is the goal of Medicaid planning. Nothing could be further from the truth. A true Medicaid plan takes everything into account, including the client's net worth and income and his ability to private pay for a nursing home should one become necessary. Regrettably, most of our clients are, through age and infirmity, unable to purchase long-term care (nursing home) insurance. Frequently the cost is too prohibitive for most predominantly middle class folks who are having trouble enough meeting their real estate taxes and other commitments.

Medicaid planning is merely a legal way of sheltering assets from a nursing home while still keeping the client (Mom or Dad or Mom and Dad) in complete control of all their assets. Stories are told of wealthy, downtown New York law firms setting up a millionaire's Medicaid plan, to make the rich client's assets disappear. In fact, there was an article published in a major newspaper which play acted a scenario whereby one high brow law firm created a plan for a millionaire so that if he went into a nursing home his assets could not be touched for his nursing home care. This simply has no basis in reality and is meant, in our opinion, for journalistic sensationalism; the wealthy clients can private pay for their nursing home stay from their income and assets, or they can afford a long-term care policy.

It is the middle class which is being devastated by Medicaid; they have too much money to qualify for Medicaid, yet are not wealthy enough to private pay. They are the ones who get financially wiped out. Medicaid planning is both legal and moral; the myriad of complex rules and regulations makes it so that most general practice attorneys simply don't know how to construct a Medicaid plan, be it for a loved one already residing in a nursing home (crisis planning), or for Mom and Dad who are both in relatively good health (non-crisis planning).

Medicaid planning deals with saving assets for clients, as well as exploring with them long-term care policies to pay for their nursing home stay. The wealthy do not need a Medicaid plan since they can private pay forever. The average person needs to plan for the nursing home contingency.

In picking an Elder Law attorney, make sure that you turn to a qualified professional who only does this type of planning, not a lawyer who merely dabbles in it. Check resumes and references; ask if they have ever been sued in malpractice; ask what they have done for their own parents. Ask how long they have been in practice and just how much of their work is in Medicaid planning. See what honors and awards the lawyer may have gotten either scholastically or from independent groups such as Bar Associations or Senior's groups. Shop around diligently.

The bottom line is that between word of mouth and public information (usually in the form of seminars or the Internet), you will arrive at the correct lawyer for you and your family.

Chapter 3:

Who Should Read this Book

In our first book, "Alzheimer's Disease: Fighting for Financial Survival," we delineated a whole group of people we felt could benefit from our book. Although we found many folks did benefit from reading it, we were surprised at the many who either did not read it or read it and didn't fully understand it. It perplexes us that any health care providers would not be keenly interested in how they could best help their patients and families of their patients save their life savings. It perplexes us how any family faced with the loss of their entire life savings to a nursing home would not want to read and fully absorb the contents of a book such as this. Remarkably, we have had folks read the book who still insist that there is a three- or five-year wait to shelter assets from a nursing home. The attitude almost seems to be that somehow we are putting one over on the government by, at best, exploiting legal techniques, or, at worst, using non-legal techniques. We find it intriguing when we hear that any loophole to help save millionaires millions of dollars is obviously legal and legitimate, whereas a loophole which might save a widow her home does not share that same air of legitimacy. The techniques and procedures set forth in this book are not for millionaires, as millionaires do not need Medicaid planning, but they are all legal, legitimate and time tested to work. With this as a prelude, we believe that this book is must reading for (1) all health care providers who care for folks just before they enter nursing homes, (2) families of loved ones afflicted with an injury, illness or disease which might lead to their confinement in a nursing home and (3) lawyers who dabble in this area of law and are "sitting targets" for malpractice suits which, we see, are the next great wave of litigation against attorneys.

A.   All Health Care Providers in Contact with Those at Risk of a Nursing Home Stay

We have been pleasantly surprised at the reception our books, pamphlets and other reading materials have received in the medical community. Virtually every hospital in our area of practice has in-house seminars to better educate their social workers and case managers about the rights of their patients. In addition, we have received a very strong interest from family physicians about the book and our informational seminars and materials. And, why not? After all, while the family may suspect or even know that something is not right with their spouse or parent, unless such spouse or parent is hospitalized or otherwise under treatment, the job falls to the family physician to refer their client out for further testing to see if Alzheimer's, Parkinson's or Multiple Sclerosis is the appropriate diagnosis. The social workers and case managers at the hospital or rehabilitation centers are on the front line. They see up close the dramatic and often tragic results of the aforesaid diseases, as well as strokes, heart attacks and cancer. In the hands of these professionals, the information provided in this book can be a financial lifeline to the families they are assisting.

B. Families of Loved Ones Afflicted with an Injury, Illness or Disease which might Lead to their Confinement in a Nursing Home

It is always a puzzle to us that folks in time of medical need, often in times of medical crisis, and often on the very brink of entering a nursing home, or sometimes already patients of a nursing home, do not scream out to read this book. We are often told by the patient's family: "We thought it was too late to do anything." The problem is that these folks at this time of personal crisis are getting this bad information from well meaning friends, neighbors and, regrettably, even from misinformed attorneys (often the family's general practice attorney). The government has done such an excellent job of convincing people that nothing can be within three or five years in advance of a nursing home stay, when nothing can be further from the truth.

As you will read further in this book, we routinely draft Medicaid plans which serve to immediately save assets for a family—assets that would have been long wiped out had we had to wait three years or five years. It is not uncommon for an adult child to meet with us to explain that Mom is in a nursing home and only has $60,000 in assets. Such child often says, "At the rate of $6,000 per month, we know Mom's money will run out well before three years, so we know you can't save anything for the family." Imagine that family's surprise when we draft a trust which protects that money in a matter of months and, if Mom is competent, that Mom can control the trust. The largest impediment to assisting folks with a loved one in crisis in a nursing home, or about to enter a nursing home, is the belief that nothing can be done because it is too late. Unless that client is on Medicaid, it is virtually never too late to save assets from a nursing home; even in cases where one spouse is on Medicaid, steps can and should be taken to protect the family's assets should the second spouse also enter a nursing home. Saving the family home is particularly an option to be used at this juncture.

C. Lawyers Who Dabble in this Area of Law

As this book is being written, we have in our office no less than three matters which allege lawyer malpractice and ask for our law firm's involvement, either as lawyers representing the plaintiffs or as expert witnesses. In two of those cases, relatively easy Medicaid plans could have been implemented, but the lawyer committed a very basic mistake. In one case, a deed of the family house from a father and mother to a daughter would have been perfectly fine (and would have saved the house from Medicaid) had the deed been first from the father to the mother and then from the mother to the daughter. The failure to take this one extra step caused the house to be forfeited by the family and a charge of Medicaid fraud brought against the daughter for failure to disclose a transfer. In this day and age of super technical interpretation and laws and regulations pertaining to Medicaid we question why any attorney would even consider dabbling in this area.

Chapter 4:

Basic Estate Planning: Wills, Trusts, Powers of Attorney and Advance Directives

A. Wills and Trusts

It is with basic estate planning that we begin our exploration of the techniques of asset protection. Just as you cannot build a solid house without a foundation, you cannot build a solid Medicaid Plan without first doing basic estate planning. Sheltering assets from the nursing home will be easier and more effective if certain basic estate planning documents have been put in place in advance.

A will, as is commonly known, is a legal document that passes assets to the heirs on death. What most people don't know about the will, however, is that before the assets are distributed to the heirs, the will needs to go through a process known as probate. All states have different probate laws, but, in large part, probate operates as follows: First, the will is filed with the court, along with a petition for appointment of the executor. (Most people think that the person you name as executor automatically becomes executor on your death. In fact, the court has to formally appoint the executor.) The judge then determines whether the will is valid. Assuming that it is, the judge then sets the amount of the bond, if required, and after the bond is filed, appoints the executor by issuing "letters of administration."

The executor then makes an inventory of all of the assets to be probated, and reports that inventory to the court. The inventory stays on file with the court, and becomes a matter of public record. Next, the executor liquidates the assets and pays the decedent's final debts and expenses. He also files any inheritance or income tax returns that may be necessary. If there are any inheritance taxes, the executor, before closing the estate, needs to obtain a "closing letter," *i.e.*, a document from the taxing authorities stating that all taxes are paid. At the end of the probate proceedings, before the assets can be distributed to the heirs, the executor makes a report to the judge of all that he has done, as well as a report of the income and expenditures of the estate. This report is known as an "accounting." It is only after the judge approves of the accounting that the assets can be distributed to the heirs.

In those states that have adopted a law known as "The Uniform Probate Code," probate is fairly straightforward. In those states which have not adopted this law, probate can be expensive, time consuming and cumbersome. In such states, it is not unusual for probate to last a year to a year and a half. Regardless of whether your state is a Uniform Probate Code state or not, probate is open to the public, meaning that the will is a public document, as is the identity of the beneficiaries and possibly, what they are inheriting.

In order to avoid the delay, expense and publicity of probate, in recent years people have been turning in increasing numbers to the "living trust," or "revocable trust." The revocable trust is a method of avoiding probate on death. Stripped to its basics, a revocable trust essentially is a glorified will. In large part, the trust says the same thing as a will, *i.e.,* who is going to inherit the assets, and who the administrator will be. The crucial difference between the two, however, is that the will is subject to probate upon death, whereas the trust is not. (As we will see in a later chapter, the revocable trust can be written with "Medicaid Triggers," that can go a very long way in sheltering assets from long-term care. A will cannot contain such provisions.) A trust has three parties: the "grantor," who is the person who sets up the trust, the "trustee," who is the person who manages the trust, and the "beneficiary," who is the person (or persons) who will get the benefit from the trust assets. When you set up a living trust, or revocable trust, you wear all three hats, that of grantor, trustee and beneficiary. You place your assets in the name of the trust, and then go about your business as usual. When you die, or if you become incompetent, a successor trustee of your choice, usually one or two of your children, takes over management of the trust. Ultimately, at your death, the beneficiaries you have named in the trust will inherit the trust assets without probate proceedings. In almost all cases, there are no legal fees to settle the trust, and settlement of your estate proceeds quickly and privately. Years ago, it was mainly the wealthy who set up trusts, while most other people had wills. These days, living trusts have become standard estate planning tools for people of moderate means, not just the wealthy.

A word about inheritance taxes is in order. Most people are pleasantly surprised to learn that there are no income taxes on an inheritance. (The exception is with retirement plans such as IRAs, 401(k)s, and the like. When these go to the spouse there are no income taxes, but when they go to the children, there are income taxes.) Estates under $1 million in value are not subject to any federal estate taxes, but those over $1 million in value are. (The $1 million threshold is slowly rising, so that by 2009 it will be $3.5 million, and by 2010 the tax will be repealed entirely. Curiously, however, unless Congress acts otherwise, the tax will be reinstated at the $1 million level in 2011.) States may have their own inheritance taxes, but these are beyond the scope of this book.

Whether you opt for a will or a living trust in your estate plan, you need to know that in the case of someone with a chronic illness that might put him in a nursing home, these documents need to be drafted with some very special provisions. Most wills and trusts contain "I love you," or "sweetheart," provisions, which leave all of the assets to the surviving spouse. Of course, in the usual case, such arrangements are entirely appropriate, but they are very definitely not appropriate where a chronic, debilitating illness is involved. In most cases, the ill party, such as someone with Alzheimer's Disease, for example, will be the first to die; however, what if this is not the case?

Consider John and Deb. They prepared a living trust which leaves all of the assets to each other, and then, on the second death, to the children. John has developed Alzheimer's, and eventually is admitted to the nursing home. John and Deb spend down their assets (the spend-down is explained in Chapter 5) and Deb is left with, say, $75,000. Unable to cope with the stress of having her husband in a nursing home, and, on top of that, with having lost most of her money, Deb suffers a heart attack and dies before John. When this happens, the trust (or the will, as the case may be) leaves everything to John. John, who is incompetent and in a nursing home, now has the $75,000. He will immediately lose his Medicaid coverage, and will have to spend down the $75,000! It is likely that the children will receive nothing. The tragedy is that with appropriate adjustments to the will or trust, this result could have been avoided, and most, if not all of the assets, could have been protected.

What should John and Deb have done? As soon as John and Deb received the Alzheimer's diagnosis, they should have amended their estate planning documents to provide that, should Deb be the first to die, the assets would pass to the children, and not to John. Alternatively, they could have prepared a special kind of trust, known as a "testamentary trust." Under this device, John could have received the benefits of the funds, but in a way that sheltered them from the Medicaid authorities. John and Deb should also have amended the beneficiary designations on their life insurance and IRAs in the same way.

However, is it as easy as "disinheriting" John in the event that Deb were to die first? Not really. Many states have statutes which prohibit the complete disinheriting of a spouse. Typically, the spouse is entitled to a portion of the estate, usually a third. This third is known as the "Elective Share" or "Statutory Share." Depending on your state, the situation can be even more complicated. Some states prohibit you from disinheriting your spouse by will, but might allow it, in part, by a trust. Of the states that have these Elective Share laws on the books, some enforce them, and others do not. Obviously, in order to properly structure your will or trust to shelter as much of the assets as possible, you should consult with an Elder Law attorney who is familiar with these laws, and how they are enforced.

Assume that John and Deb live in a state that strictly enforces the spouse's Elective Share. Deb can write a will or trust that says that John is entitled to his Elective Share, *i.e.*, one third, and no more. In this way, should Deb die first, then at least two-thirds of her estate will be preserved for the children. However, with proper planning, even in this situation, more than two-thirds can be saved. If John and Deb were savvy enough to sign the appropriate type of durable power of attorney, and Deb were to die first, then, as illustrated above, the children would get two-thirds, and John would get one-third. The children, as Attorneys-in-Fact under the durable power of attorney, could then engage in what is known as Half-a-Loaf planning, (explained in Chapter 6), in which half of John's third could be protected. Then, only one-sixth of the estate would go to the nursing home!

As you can see, you need to do basic estate planning before you can shelter assets, and you need to refine the estate plan in the case in which someone has Alzheimer's or a similar chronic illness.

B. Financial and Medical Powers of Attorney

Someone who has become mentally incompetent, due to Alzheimer's or for any other reason, lacks the legal capacity to transact any type of business, such as paying bills, signing tax returns, or buying or selling property. When an incompetent person has not done adequate estate planning, someone such as a spouse or adult child must petition the probate court for "legal guardianship." A legal guardian appointed by the court has the ability to transact business for an incompetent person. The problem with a guardianship petition, as with probate of a will after death, is that it can be time consuming, expensive and cumbersome. The attorneys must be paid, you need to testify in court and buy a bond, and you must make periodic reports to the court as to all financial transactions.

Most significantly for our purposes, a guardianship can completely destroy your ability to shelter assets from the cost of long-term care. That is, in order to be able to implement any of the asset protection strategies described in later chapters of this book, such as the Half-a-Loaf, Private Annuity, Life Estate Deed, Special Power of Appointment Deed, and others, the guardian must obtain prior permission of the probate court. The problem is that it might be unlikely that the probate court will grant permission for the guardian to do any of these things, as the role of the probate judge is to "preserve" the assets for use by the incapacitated person, even if such "preservation" means depletion by payments to the nursing home! Certainly, most people would want to save their assets for use by their spouse, and would want to leave their children a modest inheritance, but seeing to these obvious, common-sense intentions is not the role of the probate court. The court's role is to see to it that the person's assets are used for their care, even if the spouse is impoverished and the inheritance is lost, and that Medicaid is used as a last resort.

Since most people are of the opposite viewpoint, and want their assets preserved for their families and not spent on the nursing home, they would be well advised to structure their affairs to avoid guardianship proceedings. The way to do this would be to prepare a document known as a "Durable Power of Attorney" (DPOA). If you become incompetent, the holder of your Durable Power of Attorney (called the "Attorney-in-Fact") can transact your business for you, much as a guardian would do, but without reporting to the probate court.

If you insert Medicaid Planning provisions in the DPOA, (discussed in later chapters), then the Attorney-in-Fact would be able to act to shelter assets for you. Consider Jeannie and her daughter, Erica. Jeannie has an estate of about $400,000. Jeannie has a stroke, and will need nursing home care for the rest of her life. Jeannie did not have the foresight to prepare a DPOA, so Erica needs to apply to the court for guardianship. As guardian, all she is authorized to do is pay the nursing home bills each month, and see her mother's life savings be slowly whittled away as she languishes in a nursing home bed. Now let's assume that Jeannie had signed a DPOA while she was healthy, naming Erica as Attorney-in-Fact. The DPOA contains a provision allowing Erica to make gifts to herself. As we will see from a later chapter, Erica, as Attorney-in-Fact, can use a common Medicaid Planning technique that will shelter, in this case, approximately $200,000.

It is important to note that not all DPOAs are created equal. Most DPOAs do not contain Medicaid Planning provisions, so that, if you want these provisions in your DPOA, you need to consult with an attorney who is knowledgeable in the field of Medicaid law. For the same reason, it is extremely foolhardy simply to sign a form DPOA from a stationery store or computer program. Consultation with an appropriate attorney will be worth the price — remember Jeannie and Erica and the $200,000 that potentially can be saved.

C. *Advance Directives*

In addition to a DPOA, it is very important for the chronically ill person, or anyone, for that matter, to sign a Medical Power of Attorney and a Living Will. Also known as "Advance Directives," these documents deal with medical decisions and end-of-life decisions. (These are discussed in a later chapter.) Essentially, the Medical Power of Attorney allows your spouse or children to make medical decisions for you if you are unable to do so on your own. If you do not have a Medical Power of Attorney, and you become incompetent, then your family would need to seek a court guardianship. Clearly, signing the Medical Power of Attorney will avoid lengthy and potentially costly court proceedings in time of crisis.

Similarly, the Living Will, for those who believe in it, should be done at the same time. The Living Will is the document that directs the removal of life-sustaining treatment in a situation where you are terminally ill, with no hope of recovery. While both of these documents are easy to do, care should be taken to use the proper form. Each state has its own forms for advance directives, which may be obtained free of charge from hospitals. Avoid the temptation to use a form from a magazine or computer program, as it might not be recognized in your state.

Chapter 5:

The Medicaid Rules

A. The Difference Between Medicare and Medicaid

Most people believe that Medicare and Medicare Supplement insurance policies pay for a long-term nursing home stay. Unfortunately, the people who have this belief and who later enter a nursing home are in for a very unpleasant and expensive surprise. That is, Medicare, the basic health insurance program available to anyone who is disabled or who is over 65 and has paid into the Social Security system, is not designed to cover a long-term nursing home stay. Medicare covers skilled nursing home care in full for the first 20 days. From day 21 to 100, Medicare pays, subject to a deductible of approximately $100 per day, and then only on the condition that the recipient be making improvement in his condition. The deductible is paid either privately by the patient, or by his Medicare Supplement insurance policy. Once the patient stops making improvement, Medicare and the Medicare Supplement insurance stop paying, even if this occurs before expiration of the hundred days. (An appeal process is available for those who want to contest the decision to terminate Medicare prior to expiration of the hundred-day period.)

Thus, Medicare is not designed to cover long-term nursing home stays. Of course, people with mid- to late-stage Alzheimer's Disease, or people with any degenerative disease or chronic condition, are not improving. At best, their condition is stable, and at worst, it is regressing. Therefore, the care that these people need is not designed to improve their condition, but just to manage it. Such care typically deals with assistance in the so-called, "activities of daily living," such as dressing, eating, bathing, grooming, using the bathroom and the like. When a person's ability to manage the activities of daily living degenerates to such a level that he can no longer live independently, then he often enters a nursing home. Unfortunately, neither Medicare nor Medicare Supplement insurance covers nursing home level of care. Therefore, Medicare simply is not a method of payment for long-term nursing home care.

B. Three Ways of Paying for Nursing Home Care

Since Medicare will not cover the cost of a nursing home, what will? There are three ways to pay for a nursing home: long-term care insurance, private payment, and Medicaid.

1. Long-Term Care Insurance

Long-term care insurance is a type of health insurance that will pay for prolonged nursing home stays, provided that the conditions of the insurance policy are met. Depending on the policy, payment can be for as little as two years, or, more commonly, for three years, or for as long as a lifetime. The insurance can pay anywhere from a minimal amount of the nursing home charges, all the way to payment in full. The more comprehensive insurance policies

come with an "inflation rider," which states that the benefit paid rises a set percentage each year. Some policies also
include payment for home health care. Since nursing home
insurance decreases people's reliance on Medicaid, the government is enacting policies that encourage people to buy
this insurance. Recent congressional legislation, for example, makes the premiums for certain policies deductible in
part as medical expenses. (Currently, the maximum allowable deduction ranges from $240 per year for people aged
40 or less, to $2,990 for people over age 70.) Some state
laws also provide that, if you have long-term care insurance
and later need Medicaid assistance, the state will not put a
lien on your house. (The topic of Medicaid liens will be discussed in a later part of this book.)

While the use of long-term care insurance is to be
encouraged, such insurance is not for everyone, for two
reasons. First, long-term care insurance tends to be costly,
and many senior citizens, especially those on fixed
incomes, cannot afford the premiums. Generally, the
younger the age at which one purchases the insurance, the
lower the cost. (Of course, the younger the age at which
you buy the insurance, the longer you pay the premiums.)
Second, not everyone qualifies for the insurance; just like
life insurance, in which the company has the right to reject
an applicant due to his medical condition, a health insurance company has the right to set standards as to whom it
will insure. Thus, depending on a person's health, he
might not meet the underwriting standards set by the
insurance company, and thus might not qualify for the
insurance. Since, generally, younger people have fewer
health problems than older people, younger people usual-

ly are more readily approved for the insurance than are older people.

When considering nursing home insurance, it is advisable to comparison shop, as the premiums and coverage items differ between insurance companies. It is also important to know the difference between an insurance agent and an insurance broker. An insurance agent represents only one insurance company, and therefore can only sell you a policy issued by that company, even if that policy is not the best one available for you. An insurance broker, on the other hand, represents more than one company. Therefore, a broker is able to shop around the various insurance companies he represents for the policy that suits you best. In this regard, a very useful booklet called "A Shopper's Guide to Long-Term Care Insurance," can be obtained from the National Association of Insurance Commissioners, at 1-800-842-3600.

Additionally, it is important to know that nursing home insurance policies, just like other insurance policies, are complicated and are not easy to read. Typically, such policies carry what is known as a "free-look" period. The free-look period is a period of time, such as ten or twenty days from the time the policy is delivered to you, within which you can cancel it and obtain a refund. Due to the technical nature of these policies, you would be well served to read your policy very carefully, and perhaps have a qualified attorney review it, during the free-look period.

2. *Private Payment*

Nursing home insurance is a fairly new product, and comparatively few people have it. Therefore, the second way of paying for the nursing home, private payment, is usually what people resort to first. The problem here, of course, is that nursing homes are *extremely* expensive. It is not unusual for a nursing home to cost upwards of $7,000 per month, and very few people can support such a monthly payment without quickly exhausting their savings. Two common misconceptions are that a nursing home will take all of your savings in a lump sum, or will put an attachment on your house. Neither are accurate. Rather, paying for a nursing home is like paying for any other service. You receive a bill each month. Most people start out as private paying patients, and then exhaust their savings. When this happens, they turn to the next method of financing the nursing home, Medicaid. There are some continuing care facilities for which you pay a very large entry fee, possibly more than $100,000, and then a monthly fee. (These are known as continuing care retirement communities.) In exchange for accepting this payment, these facilities promise to take care of you for the rest of your life, regardless of your need. All of these facilities are somewhat different in their policies, and the terms of their agreements are spelled out in their admissions contracts. If you are considering residing in one of these facilities for yourself or for a loved one, it is essential to have a competent attorney review the contract in advance.

3. *Medicaid*

When the private pay money runs out, Medicaid takes over. Medicaid is a federal program that is administered by the states pursuant to complex regulations. The cost of Medicaid is shared by the federal, state and sometimes county governments. In some states, Medicaid is referred to as "Title 19," as it is derived from Title 19 of the Social Security Act. (Medicaid has no relation to Social Security, however.)

a. *Applying for Medicaid*

In order to qualify for Medicaid, you must meet certain medical and financial requirements. First, you must either live in a nursing home or have a medical need that requires nursing home care. In order to establish medical need, you must undergo a medical assessment, which is usually conducted by an employee of the Medicaid department or a private contractor acting on behalf of that department. Establishing medical need usually is not a problem, since only people who need nursing home care go into nursing homes. However, as state Medicaid budgets tighten, some states are making the medical criteria more and more strict.

Applications for Medicaid benefits are filed with the Medicaid office covering the geographical area in which the applicant lives. Every state handles its application process differently. Some states require that a representative of the applicant, either a spouse or holder of a durable power of attorney, appear at a personal interview, and some states handle the application process entirely by mail. Whatever the state procedure, the key to filing a successful Medicaid application is in providing the "verifications," or documentation, required. At a minimum, you will have to provide the following:

1. Proof of residence, with a copy of your deed or lease.

2. Proof of age and citizenship, with a copy of birth or baptismal certificate or naturalization certificate. If none of these can be found, a town or city voter registration card will usually suffice.
3. Social Security, Medicare and private health insurance cards. If there is private health insurance, then a copy of a current bill will also be required.
4. Marriage certificate, for married applicants.
5. Current bank account statements, and, frequently, checking statements going back one year, and sometimes three years. You will need to explain and document any large or unusual withdrawals.
6. Statement of nursing home personal needs account.
7. Life insurance policies and statement of cash value for all policies which have a combined face value of $1,500 or more.
8. Copy of durable power of attorney.
9. All trust documents, along with verification of all assets in the trust name and income derived from the trust.
10. Prepaid burial contract and cemetery deed.
11. Verification of all other financial assets, such as stocks, bonds, mutual funds, etc., and the value thereof.
12. Copies of any annuity contracts.
13. Verification of any assets transferred within the past 36 months, or 60 months in the case of a trust. This requirement applies not only to gifts, but to any asset sold within the relevant time frame. In the case of a house sale, for example, a deed and closing statement will be required.

14. Verification of all income, such as Social Security award statements and pension check stubs. For income that is direct deposited, a bank statement will do.
15. In some states, copies of tax returns.
16. Some states also require that you trace the proceeds of all accounts that have been closed, or all assets that have been sold, within the past three years.

Providing these verifications is the most tedious and difficult part of the application process. However, providing accurate verifications is of the utmost importance, as an application will not be approved until all verifications have been provided, and all issues raised by the verifications have been explained. The burden of supplying these verifications is on the applicant; the Medicaid office will not assist you in getting any documents. Further, there are fairly tight time deadlines in providing these verifications, and an application in which the verifications are not supplied within the deadlines will be denied. For this reason, it is advisable to assemble the verifications before filing the application; it also can be very helpful to be represented by a competent attorney during the application process. (The fees of the attorney can be used towards the Medicaid spenddown, to be discussed later.)

A word of caution is in order about who represents you in applying for Medicaid. Many nursing homes will offer to complete the Medicaid application for you at no charge; some nursing homes even contract with private companies, whose job it is to complete Medicaid applications for nursing home residents. It goes without saying, however, that something you get "for free" is usually worth what you pay for it. This is not to imply that nursing homes are less than competent in completing the application, as that is far from the truth. Rather, as will be explained later, a competent Elder Law attorney is working for you, with protection of your financial interests in mind, whereas the nursing home decidedly does not have your financial interests in mind. An analogy would be letting the IRS figure your income tax. Certainly the IRS will do so correctly, but isn't it wiser to do tax planning with your own CPA, whose job it is to see to it that you pay the lowest tax you legally can pay? This analogy holds true in the Medicaid process as well.

Under federal law, a Medicaid applicant can seek payments retroactive three months prior to when the application was filed. However, since the application process itself can take two to three months and sometimes longer, and since the nursing home is not being paid while application is pending, you would be well advised to start the process before running out of money, rather than after. A good rule of thumb is to file the application while you have three months' worth of private funds available. In this way, the application will probably be approved just as you are running out of money.

If you are dissatisfied with the results of the application, you can request an appeal that is known as a "fair hearing." The fair hearing is not a second chance. Rather, it is a proceeding at which you will have to prove that the caseworker wrongfully denied the application, due to a mistake of fact, or a mistake in applying the law. Fair hearings are conducted by a "hearings examiner," who is an employee of the state or of the Medicaid agency. At a fair hearing, each side will have the ability to offer evidence, present and cross examine witnesses, and state the legal basis of his or her case. Although a fair hearing is somewhat similar to a court trial, it is far less formal. The process of claiming a fair hearing is simple and informal; usually, a letter to the Medicaid caseworker who handled the application will suffice. However, there are strict time deadlines for doing so.

It is important to note that under federal law, a nursing home cannot discriminate, discharge or in any way alter the treatment of a Medicaid patient. If, shortly before a private-pay patient switches to Medicaid, the facility transfers the patient to a hospital or to another part of the facility, you have cause to investigate, and determine whether the move was medically justified. Additionally, any facility that accepts federal funds, such as Medicare or Medicaid, has no legal right to require that other family members contribute to the payment, or guarantee payment. Any contracts providing such guarantees are void.

b. *Medicaid's Financial Requirements*
1. General Rules
Medicaid law puts very strict limits on the amount and type of assets that a recipient or spouse of a recipient is allowed to have. Certain types of assets are not counted towards eligibility, and accordingly, are called "non-countable assets," whereas certain assets are countable. You are allowed to have unlimited non-countable assets, but there are limits on the countable assets you may have. Non-countable assets include, among others:

1. Your home, regardless of value, if your spouse is living and residing in the home. (In the case of a

single person, the house is fully countable.) Note that only *one* residence is exempt, so that if you have a vacation home, investment property or winter home in Florida, the non-homestead property will be countable.

2. Prepaid funeral contracts, as long as they are irrevocable, *i.e,* as long as you do not have the right to cancel the contract for a refund. Some states have limits on the amount that can be paid for the funeral. Note that the payment must be for the cost of the funeral. That is, you cannot "overpay" for the funeral, and then have your heirs get a refund of any unused amounts after the funeral.

3. One burial plot for the applicant and spouse.

4. Essential household items, such as appliances, clothing, household furnishings and personal, non-investment jewelry.

5. Property subject to legal proceedings, such as property in probate.

6. Lump sum death benefits for funeral and burial expenses.

7. Income tax refunds.

8. One motor vehicle. Some states put a cap on the value of the vehicle.

9. Cash value of life insurance policies, up to $1,500. Insurance is only exempt if the face value is below $1,500. If the face value exceeds $1,500, then the cash value is added up, and only $1,500 is exempt.

10. Term life insurance, having no cash value.

11. Cash assets up to $2,000 or $2,500, depending on the state.

All other assets are countable. Examples of countable assets are the home (in the case of unmarried applicants), bank accounts, IRAs and similar retirement accounts, cash value of life insurance above $1,500, stocks, bonds and mutual funds, second homes, second cars, deferred annuities, and anything else that can be sold or turned into cash, even if a penalty or surrender charge is involved.

If you have countable assets over the allowable limit, you will not be eligible for Medicaid until you have spent down to the limit. This process, not surprisingly, is known as the "spenddown," and is discussed later. *Alternatively, and the very point of this book, is that there are certain very powerful Medicaid Planning devices you can use to preserve most, if not all, of your countable assets, and still allow you to qualify for Medicaid.*

Medicaid has separate rules for income, which are extremely complex, arcane and defy understanding. In the case of a single person, all of the income, with certain exceptions, must be paid to the nursing home. You are allowed to keep a minimal "personal needs allowance," of $50 to $60 per month, depending on state, as well as sufficient money to pay for health insurance premiums. In the case of a married couple, the income of the healthy spouse is not counted, while the income of the institutionalized spouse is. The healthy spouse does have the benefit of certain income protections, discussed below.

2. Division of Assets for Married Couples

Under a law ironically known as the "spousal impoverishment" provisions of the Medicare Catastrophic Coverage Act of 1988, the healthy spouse benefits from certain, albeit minimal, asset protections. Unfortunately, these protections can hardly be called protections at all. In Medicaid parlance, the nursing home spouse is known as the "institutionalized spouse," and the spouse living at home is known as the "community spouse." Congress, in passing the spousal impoverishment rules, recognized that it would not be in society's interest to completely impoverish the community spouse. Under the spousal impoverishment rules, the community spouse is entitled to keep half of the couple's countable assets, up to a maximum of about $89,000. (This number rises each year with inflation.) In some states, the community spouse can keep the entire $89,000.

It makes no difference whose name the assets are in, and it makes no difference who brought the asset to the marriage. Many spouses, especially those involved in second marriages, take false comfort from the fact that they hold their assets in separate names, or from the fact that they have entered into a premarital agreement. However, when a spouse in a second marriage enters a nursing home, the community spouse is in for an extremely uncomfortable surprise: whose name the asset is in, or whether there is a premarital agreement, is completely irrelevant. When a couple says, "I do," they are, for Medicaid purposes, consenting to treat their assets as if they were jointly held, since, in the eyes of the law, the marital unit has one pocketbook. The very most that the community spouse can keep is half, but no more than the maximum of $89,000.

The "protection" provided by the spousal impoverishment law is not automatic; rather, the community spouse must request it. The procedure by which the community spouse requests this asset protection is known as a "Resource Assessment." Once the institutionalized spouse enters a hospital, or skilled or intermediate nursing facility and is likely to remain institutionalized for 30 consecutive days or more, the community spouse is entitled to have a Resource Assessment done. The Resource Assessment does not have to be done at that time. It can be done later, as part of the Medicaid application itself, after the spend-down has taken place. However, the community spouse would be well advised to do the Resource Assessment as early as possible. As the Resource Assessment is essentially a financial "snapshot" of the assets on the date of institutionalization, it is easier to get the needed financial records shortly after the fact, rather than months, or sometimes years later. This is especially true these days, when banks change names so frequently. The documentation required to process a Resource Assessment is the same as that needed for a full application, and the procedure is the same as well.

The mechanics of a Resource Assessment are as follows. The value of all countable assets are added together, and divided by two. The result, or the $89,000, whichever is lower, is called the "Community Spouse Resource Allowance," or CSRA. For couples with assets of up to approximately $34,000, the community spouse may keep a total of about $17,000 even if that amount is higher than half of the total. For those couples with assets above $34,000, the community spouse may keep half, up to a cap of approximately $89,000. (In some states, the community spouse may keep the first $89,000.)

For example, say that Andy is in the nursing home, and Wendy, his wife, lives at home. They have the following assets:

House	$150,000
CDs	100,000
Bonds	55,000
IRA	20,000
Car	15,000
Second car	5,000
Total	$345,000

Remember that the house and first car are not countable assets. Therefore, the countable assets, in this case, would be $180,000, *i.e.*, the assets above less the house and more expensive car. Of this amount, Wendy would be allowed a CSRA of $89,000 plus the home and more expensive car and Andy would be allowed to keep $2,500. As a couple, Andy and Wendy would have to spend down the rest of the assets. (As we will see later, there are certain Medicaid Planning techniques which will allow Wendy to keep most, if not all, of the assets, and still have Andy qualify for Medicaid.)

Let's take another example. Say that Roz is in the nursing home, and Rob, her husband, is the community spouse. Their assets are as follows:

House	$150,000
CDs	100,000
Car	15,000
Total	$265,000

Remember that the house and car are not countable, so that Roz and Rob's countable assets would be the $100,000 in CDs. Rob would be allowed to keep the house, car and his CSRA of $50,000. Roz would be allowed to keep $2,500, and the couple would have to spend down the rest. (As stated above, in some states, Rob would be allowed to keep the full $89,000.)

It is said that, in life, "timing is everything." The same holds true for Medicaid. Say that during the spend-down process, Rob inherits $75,000 from his parents. Unfortunately, the Resource Assessment is *not* adjusted to take the inheritance into account, and Roz and Rob would still have to spend down to the $50,000 level. In other words, Rob would not be entitled to keep any of the inheritance. (If he inherited this money after Roz was on Medicaid, however, he would be able to keep it.)

At this point we get to our first asset protection technique. Working with the children, it is possible to significantly increase the CSRA. In the above example of Roz and Rob, the countable assets are $100,000, and Rob can keep half, or $50,000. Say that the day before Roz enters the nursing home, the couple's son, Michael, lends them $78,000, and Roz and Rob sign a demand promissory note for that amount. Their assets are now $178,000. The Resource Assessment only looks at assets, *and ignores liabilities*. Thus, the debt to Michael is not counted, and all Medicaid looks at are the assets of $178,000. How or when those assets were acquired is not relevant. The Resource Assessment would then show that Rob's CSRA would be the full $89,000. After the Resource Assessment is completed, Roz and Rob repay the debt to Michael. Their assets are back to the $100,000 they started with; however, instead of being able to keep only $50,000, Rob can now keep $89,000, and the spend-down would be reduced from $50,000 to only $8,500. Here is how the math would look:

Without Loan from Michael
Total Assets	$100,000
Less Protected for Rob	(50,000)
Less Protected for Roz	(2,500)
To spend down	$47,500

With Loan from Michael
Total Assets	$178,000
Less payback	(78,000)
Less Protected for Rob	(89,000)
Less Protected for Roz	(2,500)
Spenddown	$8,500

If the community spouse does not have a child willing or able to make a loan of the type described above, or if he does not want to involve his children, then the law presents him with two ways to try and raise the CSRA. First, if he feels that the caseworker has made a mistake of fact or law, he can request a fair hearing to have the mistake corrected. Second, he can try to raise the CSRA by a sophisticated technique dealing with income. This technique is described in the next section.

3. Treatment of Income for Married Couples

We have seen how Medicaid treats assets. How does Medicaid treat income? Once the asset requirements have been met, the Medicaid authorities will then consider the income of the married couple. Subject to deductions for a small personal needs allowance ($50 to $60 per month, depending on state) and the cost of medical insurance, the income of the institutionalized spouse must be paid to the nursing home, in full. Most senior citizens live on fixed incomes, and need the incomes of both parties in order to live. Therefore, the rule that the income of the institutionalized spouse goes to the nursing home can lead to extreme financial hardship for the healthy spouse. In order to alleviate this problem somewhat, the law provides some income protections for the healthy spouse.

Depending on the couple's circumstances, the community spouse may be allowed to keep some of the income of the institutionalized spouse, instead of this income being paid to the nursing home. Under federal law, each state must establish a "Minimum Monthly Maintenance Needs Allowance," or MMMNA. The MMMNA must be at least 150% of the federal poverty line for a family of two, and it rises each year. The MMMNA currently is $1,493, but may be as high as $2,232.

If the community spouse's income is below the MMMNA of $1,493, then, depending on his housing and utility expenses, he will be entitled to an "allowance" from the income of the institutionalized spouse. A simple example will illustrate the point. Say that Stephen is the institutionalized spouse, and Millie is the community spouse. Stephen's income from Social Security and pension totals $2,000 per month, whereas Millie's income consists of Social Security of $500 per month. Millie owns her house outright, and thus has no mortgage payment. She pays

$350 per month for property taxes, $35 per month for homeowner's insurance, $100 per month for heat and electricity, and $35 per month for telephone, for a total of $520. The law provides for a standard "shelter allowance" of $447.90 which rises each year. The shelter allowance is subtracted from Millie's total expenses of $520, leaving "excess shelter" costs of $72.10. Next, the "maximum income standard" of $1,493 is added to Millie's excess shelter amount of $72.10, for a total of $1,565.10. This later sum is considered to be Millie's needs. Millie's income of $500 is subtracted from her needs of $1,565.10, leaving a difference of $1,065.10. Thus, from Steve's income of $2,000, he will be allowed his $50 personal needs allowance, plus enough money to cover his health insurance. Millie will then get an allowance of $1,065 from Steve, and the rest of his income will go to the nursing home. Conversely, if Millie's income were above the MMMNA plus the excess shelter allowance, she would not be allowed to receive any of Stephen's income, but she would be entitled to keep all of her income in full.

Even though the community spouse is entitled to receive the benefit of some income protection in the manner described above, this protection is quite minimal. That is, the formula does not take into account the needs of the community spouse for food, cable television, cell phone, clothing, prescription drugs, gasoline or any type of recreation.

Now that we have looked at Medicaid's treatment of income, we can revisit a topic from the previous section, that of increasing the Community Spouse Resource Allowance (CSRA). Recall that the CSRA is the amount of money protected for the community spouse, and is generally equal to half of the countable assets, or $89,000, whichever is less. Usually, all of the monthly income of the institutionalized spouse must be paid to the nursing home, less a personal allowance and enough money to cover health insurance. Federal law says that if the income of the community spouse is less than the MMMNA, he may request that the CSRA be raised, with the idea that the extra resources allowed him will be invested to generate sufficient income to make up for the shortfall in income.

Here is the issue, though: Is the community spouse entitled to this increase in resources based on his income alone, or only after including the income of the nursing home spouse as well?

About 30 states are "income first" states. That is, the community spouse must first take the income of the institutionalized spouse before being entitled to raise the CSRA. The alternative is the "resource first," rule, in which the CSRA can be raised without recourse to the income of the nursing home spouse. It would seem that the federal law which governs this issue requires that states use the "resource first" rule, though the law is ambiguous. In a decision released in February 2002, in the case of *Wisconsin Dep't. of Health and Family Services v. Blumer*, the US Supreme Court settled this question. The court held that federal law permitted states to use the income first approach if they so chose.

Meeting the MMMNA by raising the CSRA is extremely technical. Some states have detailed regulations governing how it is to be done, and some states' regulations do not mention it at all. In any event, if this is to be done, it needs

to be done by a fair hearing, since the Medicaid caseworker alone cannot grant it. Therefore, you will have to file a
Medicaid application, have it be denied due to excess
resources, and then claim a fair hearing to meet the
MMMNA by increasing the CSRA.

4. *The Spend-down*

Due to Medicaid's strict asset limits, many people need
to spend down their assets in order to qualify for benefits.
If you need to do this, there are certain spenddown strategies that can help you. As mentioned above, certain assets
are not countable for Medicaid purposes. Therefore, why
not try to convert countable assets into non-countable
ones? It is perfectly permissible to spend money on non-
countable assets, as long as you pay fair value for them.
For example, a prepaid funeral contract is not a countable
asset. Therefore, if Wilfred goes into the nursing home,
Tina, his wife, can buy a prepaid funeral for him and one
for herself as well. (The spenddown does not have to be for
the institutionalized spouse; the community spouse can be
the beneficiary of the spenddown.) In this way, the funeral is paid for out of the spenddown funds, *i.e.*, the funds
that would otherwise have gone to the nursing home, and
not the funds protected for the community spouse. One car
per family is also not countable. Therefore, Tina can trade
in her old car and buy a new one. Tina can also buy furni-
ture, personal items, home improvements and repairs, all
without limit, or she can pay down bills. Care should be
taken, however, not to buy items such as expensive jewelry, artwork, or a luxury car, as these items may be considered to be investments, which would then be countable.

Whether the spenddown is done by purchasing non-countable assets or by paying the nursing home (obviously the last resort), attention must be given to tax consequences. Many people today hold the bulk of their wealth in retirement assets such as IRAs and 401ks. There are significant income tax consequences when these assets are liquidated. The same is true of appreciated assets such as stocks and real estate, and assets with a taxable component, such as savings bonds and annuities. In planning the spenddown, you need to be sensitive to the income tax consequences of liquidating assets. Therefore, it is very often advisable to consult with an accountant or financial advisor prior to finalizing plans both as to the order in which assets should be liquidated and the timing of their liquidation.

Spending down in accordance with the state requirements, however, can be viewed as a last resort. We have already looked at some modest techniques which can minimize what the patient and spouse have to spend. The field of Medicaid Planning, which we discuss in the next chapter, can actually allow you to save the bulk of your wealth, or sometimes all of it, while making you eligible for Medicaid.

Chapter 6:
Medicaid Planning For Those in a Nursing Home or About to Go into One

A. The Ethics of Medicaid Planning

Medicaid Planning can be defined as structuring or repositioning your assets in a way that protects them from being depleted by the nursing home, while at the same time making yourself eligible for Medicaid benefits. Some people believe that Medicaid Planning is unethical, since it makes people eligible for public benefits which were designed for those who are impoverished. As Elder Law attorneys, we believe without hesitation, that Medicaid Planning is legal, moral and ethical. Virtually all of our clients are decent people with high ethical standards. They have saved, lived frugally, and paid their bills and taxes without complaint over a lifetime. These are the people who have made possible the success that our society now enjoys. In our view, it is completely wrong for any of these good, honest people to become impoverished merely because they have the ill fortune of needing nursing home care.

The Medicaid laws are cruelly unfair to such people. Consider the example of two senior citizens, both age 75. One person develops cancer and his treatment costs, say, $200,000. Medicare and Medicare supplement insurance will pay for most of his costs. The other person develops Alzheimer's and has to go into a nursing home. His nursing home stay will also cost $200,000, yet Medicare will pay for none of his care. Where is the justice or logic here? Why does society pay for the cancer treatment but not the Alzheimer's treatment? Is Alzheimer's a less serious disease? Is the Alzheimer's patient less worthy of society's protection than the cancer patient? Of course not, but the law would make it seem that way.

It also seems to us that Medicaid Planning is no different from tax planning. For example, it is commonly known that there are many items that you can deduct from your income tax. Mortgage payments, state and local property taxes and charitable gifts are but a few. Taking advantage of these tax deductions, however, is voluntary. If you have a mortgage, the IRS does not require you to deduct the interest and you can include it on your taxes if you want to do so. Of course, no rational person would do such a thing, because the law says that you do not have to. Medicaid Planning is no different. Congress has provided for many techniques that legally allow you to shelter your assets from long-term care, just as it has provided ways of sheltering income from taxes. Since Congress has allowed these techniques to exist, no one should be criticized for using them to his advantage. How can you criticize someone for taking advantage of the laws that Congress has put in place for his benefit? Of course, no one will force you to protect your assets with Medicaid Planning, and you are free to spend your savings on the nursing home, if you want to do so. That is a choice you and your family need to make. However, it is not right to condemn as unethical those who take advantage of what Congress has deemed to be perfectly legal.

B. A Word of Caution

The success of the techniques to be described in this chapter depends on strict adherence to very technical points of law, many of which differ from state to state, and many of which may change from time to time. Further, some of these techniques are dependent on whether the person is married or single. None of these techniques should be undertaken without representation by a knowledgeable and experienced Elder Law attorney. Most people think of lawyers as general practitioners. However true this may have been years ago, it is far from accurate today. Medicaid law is so detailed and complex, and the rules so technical, that comparatively few lawyers engage in this field of practice. In fact, while virtually all Elder Law attorneys practice in the field of estate planning, fairly few estate planning attorneys practice Elder Law. With this caveat firmly in mind, let us look at the various techniques of Medicaid Planning.

C. Medicaid Planning Based on the Transfer of Asset Rules

When it comes to Medicaid law, no technique is more misunderstood or misused than gifting assets. When used in connection with the proper kind of trust, gifting can shelter a good deal of the assets of someone who is in a nursing home, or about to go into one. When used improperly, however, gifting can cause Medicaid disqualification, extra taxes, loss of assets or worse.

First, let's clear up some common misunderstandings about gifting. The biggest misconception about gifting concerns when and under what circumstances it is advisable to make gifts. Let's say that Dianna is about to go into the nursing home. Her total assets consist of a savings account worth $30,000. She does not want to lose her life savings, so just before going into the nursing home, she makes gifts of $10,000 to each of her three sisters. What Dianna does not realize is that the fact that she made gifts within three years of applying for Medicaid has, in her case, some very severe consequences. Here, Dianna will be disqualified from Medicaid for a period of time, and if she absolutely needs to go into the nursing home immediately, she has created some very major problems for herself.

Unfortunately for Dianna, she made her gifts in ignorance of the transfer-of-asset rules. Essentially, the transfer-of-asset rules state that if a gift is made within three years of applying for Medicaid, then the donor (maker) of the gift will, as a result of the gift, be disqualified for Medicaid benefits. The disqualification will not last forever, however, but will be based on the size and timing of the gift. The larger the gift, the longer the disqualification; the smaller the gift, the shorter the disqualification. More precisely, the law states that the length of the disqualification will be equal to the size of the gift divided by the average private-pay nursing home rate in the state ("disqualification rate"). The idea is that if you gave away sufficient assets to pay for, say, six months in the nursing home, then you will be unable to qualify for Medicaid benefits for six months. If you give away sufficient assets to pay for one year, you will be disqualified for one year, and so on. Let's say, for example, that in your state, the disqualification rate is $5,000 per month. If you give away $45,000 within three years of filing for Medicaid, then you will be disqualified for benefits for nine months (*i.e.*, $45,000 divided by $5,000 = 9). Each state sets its own disqualification rate, and these rates periodically change. Unfortunately, these rates are usually significantly less than the rates actually charged by nursing homes.

Let's look at Dianna's case. Just before going into the nursing home, she gave away $30,000. In a $5,000 per month state, she has disqualified herself for Medicaid benefits for six months. She has no money to pay the nursing home, since she gave it all away, and she is disqualified from Medicaid for six months, since she made gifts improperly. Therefore, for the next six months, she is in limbo. If she cannot live independently any more, and has to go into the nursing home, she is in deep trouble.

The transfer-of-asset rule ties into another Medicaid concept, that of the lookback period. In the field of Medicaid law, there is no concept that is more misunderstood than that of the lookback period. There is a 36-month lookback period for transfers of assets (i.e., gifts) to individuals, and a 60-month lookback period for transfers to irrevocable trusts. That is, Medicaid can only ask about, or look back on, transfers to individuals that have occurred within the past 36 months, or transfers to irrevocable trusts that have occurred within the past 60 months. If you gave away an asset worth $100,000 to your son 37 months ago, Medicaid will not take the gift into account, because the gift fell outside of the lookback period. However, if you gave a $100,000 asset to your son within the 36-month lookback period, and if the monthly disqualification rate in your state is $5,000, then you will be disqualified from Medicaid for 20 months. Worse, the potential period of Medicaid disqualification is unlimited. That is, if you gave away $1,000,000, and then apply for Medicaid within the 36-month lookback, in a state that uses $4,500 as the disqualification rate, you will be disqualified from Medicaid for 222 months. If, on the other hand, you gave away $1,000,000, and then applied for Medicaid 36 months later, the gift will have been outside of the lookback period, and your maximum liability for paying the nursing home will be 36 months. As you can see, failure to comply with these technical aspects of the law can be very costly, indeed.

To sum up, the transfer of asset/lookback rule contains an *if* and a *then*, and can be stated as follows: If you gave away an asset during the relevant lookback period, then, based on how much you gave away, and when you gave it away, you will be disqualified for Medicaid for a certain number of months.

1. Exceptions to the Transfer of Asset Rules

There are a number of exceptions to the transfer-of-asset rule. For example, a transfer to avoid foreclosure is not penalized. Neither is a transfer of the home under these circumstances:

1. A transfer to a spouse;

2. A transfer to a child who is blind or permanently or totally disabled;

3. A transfer to a sibling who has an equity interest in the home, (i.e., whose name is on the deed) and who resided there for at least one year prior to the individual's admission to the nursing home;

4. A transfer to a child over 21 who lived in the house and provided care to the parent, such that the parent was kept out of the nursing home for two years.

Let's look at No. Four more carefully, since this exception to the transfer of asset rule is very important. Known as the "caretaker child exception," it can help to shelter the house in the right circumstance. Say that Rita, a widow, has a medical condition that prevents her from living independently. In fact, her condition is so severe that she needs permanent nursing home care. Fortunately for Rita, however, her son, Maurice, lives at home with her. Maurice, who is fervently dedicated to his mother, takes care of her seven days a week, and is thus able to keep her out of a nursing home. If Maurice keeps Rita out of the nursing home for two years, and if Rita's doctor will so state in writing, then Rita can transfer the house to Maurice, and will not be subject to a Medicaid transfer-of-asset penalty.

The policy behind this rule is clear; it encourages adult children to keep their parents out of the nursing home by rewarding them with a gift of the house, thereby saving the Medicaid system for paying for two years' worth of nursing home care. The caretaker child exception is interpreted literally. The child needs to live in the house; living in a mobile home on the same property will not suffice; nor will living in a different apartment in the same building.

Further, the child must actually have provided the care himself, and not hired someone else to do it. However, in the right circumstances, this rule can be extremely useful in sheltering the house. As you can see, the transfer-of-asset rules, and the exceptions thereto, are extremely technical and are full of traps for the unwary. In the next section, we will see in another way how we can use these rules to our advantage.

2. *Paying for the Full Three-Year Lookback Period*

The transfer-of-asset rules we have just examined lead to two powerful Medicaid planning devices which can save the family many thousands of dollars. Both of these devices work for people who are in a nursing home now, or who are about to go into one. First, if you are fortunate enough to be able to pay privately for three years' worth of care, then you can gift out all of your assets above that amount. These days, three years in a nursing home could be expected to cost some $240,000. Thus, one Medicaid Planning technique would be to escrow $240,000 to cover payments required to fund the 36-month lookback period. All assets above that level can be safely gifted away.

As discussed shortly, however, to whom you make the gift is crucial. You almost never want to gift your money or other assets to your adult children, because the assets are then subject to the children's liabilities. For example, say your assets are $450,000. You keep $240,000 on hand to cover three years' worth of nursing home payments, and gift your daughter $210,000. She later gets divorced, and your ex son-in-law claims a part of that money as part of the property settlement. Or worse, say your daughter dies before you, and has a will which leaves the money to her husband, whom you never trusted. He inherits your money, remarries a woman with two children, and moves to a different part of the country. Your life savings will undoubtedly pay for his wife's new car and his stepchildren's college education. Or, let's say you gift money to your son, and he loses his job and needs to declare bankruptcy. Your money will go to his creditors. We need not say more, since, as you can see, gifting money to your adult children is fraught with difficulties, uncertainties and loss of control and creditor issues. If you need the money back, you might not be able to get it back. Therein lies the importance of the Gift Trust, discussed next.

3. The Half-a-Loaf and Gift Trust

The most powerful Medicaid Planning tool ever derived is known as the Half-a-Loaf. With the Half-a-Loaf, it is possible to shelter approximately half of the assets, even if the person *is already in the nursing home, or about to go into one.* That is, taking into account the person's assets, income, expenses and the disqualification rate in effect in your state, it is possible to calculate the amount of money needed to cover the period of Medicaid disqualification caused by a lump-sum gift. Factoring in all of these variables, it is generally possible, with a Half-a-Loaf, to shelter between 40 and 60 percent of the person's assets. To take a simple example, say the assets are $100,000, and the state's disqualification rate is $5,000. A gift of $50,000 is made, which will disqualify the nursing home patient from benefits for 12 months. The remaining $50,000 will, roughly speaking, be sufficient to cover the next 12 months' worth of nursing home charges. At the end of the 12-month period, the applicant will be Medicaid eligible.

Of course, in real life, the analysis is much more complex. Take Phil, for example. Phil lives in a state in which the Medicaid disqualification rate is $5,000 per month. However, Phil's monthly nursing home bill is actually $6,500 and is increasing at the rate of five percent per year. On top of that, he pays $250 per month for health insurance, $175 per month for prescriptions, $25 for cable television, $30 for newspaper subscriptions and $20 for haircuts. He gets Social Security income of $875 and a pension of $550. Say Phil has $200,000. In order to calculate how much of Phil's $200,000 can be sheltered with the Half-a-Loaf, you need to factor in all of these variables, as well as account for a reasonable rate of inflation and taxes incurred on the liquidation of assets. Taking all of these factors into account, the Half-a-Loaf can shelter approximately $95,000 out of Phil's $200,000. If Phil were to do nothing, the nursing home would get all of his money.

As can be seen, Half-a-Loaf planning can be, without doubt, the most significant Medicaid Planning technique available. In fact, Half-a-Loaf planning is so powerful that Congress once tried to end it. On January 1, 1997, the Health Insurance Portability and Accountability Act of 1996 came into effect. Section 217 of the Act stated that, "[Anyone who] knowingly and willfully disposes of assets (including by any transfer in trust) in order for an individual to become eligible for medical assistance...if disposing of the assets results in the imposition of a period of ineligibility for such assistance..." shall be guilty of a crime. Popularly referred to as the "Granny Goes to Jail Law," the statute shortly came under heavy criticism from senior's groups, legal scholars and the bar. The result was that the law was amended so as to exonerate clients from criminal responsibility, but to impose criminal penalties on paid advisors (*i.e.*, Elder Law attorneys) who counseled clients about the disposal of assets during the disqualification period.

Fortunately, attorneys and clients no longer have to worry about this criminal statute. In March 1998, Attorney General Janet Reno, in a letter to then Speaker of the House Newt Gingrich, advised that the Justice Department would not be enforcing the statute, due to serious questions about its constitutionality. At the same time, the New York State Bar Association sued the federal government, alleging that the law was unconstitutional. Ultimately, on September 14, 1998, the Federal District Court found that the law was indeed unconstitutional on First Amendment grounds, and entered a permanent injunction against the Justice Department from enforcing it. Therefore, the law, having been declared unconstitutional and invalidated by the courts, is no longer a cause for concern.

Frequently, Half-a-Loaf planning is done by one of the adult children acting as power of attorney for the disabled parent. In this case, extreme care must be used in how the Half-a-Loaf is structured. The law states that an attorney-in-fact under a power of attorney has the highest duties of care and loyalty to the creator of the power of attorney. In other words, as attorney-in-fact, you cannot take any chances whatsoever with the funds to which you are entrusted. Therefore, in order to avoid the liability problems referred to above, and to avoid any claim of conflict-of-interest or commingling funds, neither of which an attorney-in-fact is permitted to do, it is very important to use the Half-a-Loaf in conjunction with an appropriate type of creditor protection trust. We call this trust the Gift Trust.

Even in situations in which a Half-a-Loaf is not done under a power of attorney, but is done by the disabled person making a direct gift, it needs to be done with extreme care. That is, in order to avoid the problems inherent in making large gifts to your adult children (liability, loss of control, death or divorce of the children), it is essential that the recipient of the gift not hold the funds in his own name, but place them into the Gift Trust. Such a trust will not die, will not get divorced or remarried, be sued or declare bankruptcy. Think of the Gift Trust as a protective wrapper around your money, safeguarding it from your children's creditors, ex-spouses (or current spouses, for that matter) or whatever other financial trouble your children might get into.

Let us see how the Gift Trust works in conjunction with the Half-a-Loaf, whether done under power of attorney or by the disabled person directly. First, the amount of money that can be sheltered with the Half-a-Loaf is calculated, and these funds are gifted to one or more of the beneficiaries. Doing so will result in a three-year lookback period, as opposed to the five-year trust lookback period. The beneficiaries then place these assets into the Gift Trust. The Gift Trust needs to be an irrevocable trust, *i.e.,* a trust which neither the trustees nor the beneficiaries can change. That is, a revocable trust would be subject to creditors, while an irrevocable trust is not. When the Medicaid recipient passes away the trust is terminated, and the funds within the trust are distributed to the beneficiaries. The state has no right to make a claim against these funds and if the funds are under $1 million, which is usually the case, they are inherited tax free.

Usually, though not always, the Gift Trust names two trustees, who must act jointly. Thus, in order to withdraw funds from the trust, or to move funds between investments within the trust, both signatures would be required. The trust also contains provisions which curtail access to funds of any beneficiary who is subject to defaulted liabilities or who is being sued or divorced. In these important ways, the Half-a-Loaf and Gift Trust completely protect the assets. The Half-a-Loaf protects the assets from the nursing home, and the Gift Trust further protects the assets from the liabilities of the beneficiaries.

The Gift Trust must also follow, to the letter, the terms stated in the nursing home patient's will. For example, let's say that Aunt Pat is in the nursing home suffering from Alzheimer's and niece Joanne holds the power of attorney. After consultation with the Elder Law attorney, it is determined that a Half-a-Loaf is appropriate and that $75,000 can be sheltered. Aunt Pat has no children, but has three nieces, Joanne, Valerie and Marilyn. All three nieces are beneficiaries of Aunt Pat's will. If Joanne makes the gift of $75,000 to herself and she dies before Aunt Pat, then the $75,000 is going to pass through Joanne's will to her own husband or children. What happens to Valerie and Marilyn? They are out the money, and they would have to sue Joanne's heirs in order to obtain their share. Obviously, we want to avoid this situation. Therefore,

Joanne should put the Half-a-Loaf funds into a Gift Trust naming Joanne, Valerie and Marilyn as equal beneficiaries, just as Aunt Pat's will states. After Aunt Pat goes onto Medicaid, the trust money is safe and after she dies, the three nieces inherit the funds.

4. Tax Consequences

Before leaving the topic of gifting, an explanation of the tax consequences of gifting needs to be made. Most people know that you can gift $11,000 to anyone per year without any tax consequences. (For many years, this amount was $10,000. In 2002 it went up to $11,000.) However, very few people understand the tax consequences of making gifts above this amount. Luckily, in most Medicaid Planning cases, there will be absolutely no income or gift tax consequences. First, it is important to understand that there is no income tax whatsoever on a gift. If you are fortunate enough to receive, say, a gift of $500,000 (or any amount, for that matter), you do not need to report the gift on your income tax return. Rather, interestingly enough, the tax burden falls on the person who makes the gift. The donor of a gift of above $11,000 to any person in any one year must report the gift by April 15 of the following year on IRS Form 709, a Gift Tax Return. Fortunately, however, each citizen has a lifetime gifting limit, tax free, of $1,000,000. Therefore, even though a gift of over $11,000 needs to be reported to the IRS, it will be free of tax. Naturally, almost all Half-a-Loaf transactions involve far less than these amounts. While these transactions need to be reported to the IRS, they will be free of federal tax. Of course, each state has its own rules regarding the taxability of gifts, which are beyond the scope of this book.

5. Immediate Annuity

Equal in power to the Half-a-Loaf is a certain type of annuity known as an immediate annuity. When you purchase an immediate annuity, you transfer a sum of money, usually to an insurance company, in exchange for monthly payments of principal and interest back to you. Think about a promissory note. With a promissory note, you transfer a sum of money to a borrower. In exchange, the borrower pays you back in monthly installments of principal and interest. The most significant difference between a promissory note and an immediate annuity, however, concerns the length of the payment term. With a promissory note, the payments can be for any length of time agreed to by lender and borrower. With an immediate annuity, the length of payment term is based on the life expectancy of the person who contributed the money.

The beauty of an immediate annuity is that, properly used, it can shelter large amounts of money, *sometimes as much as 100%,* from long-term care. Let's see how immediate annuities can be used, first for a single person, then for a married couple. Sue, never married, is going into a nursing home. She is 75 years old, and has $100,000 in assets. If she merely spends her money on the nursing home, it will be exhausted in, say, a year and a half. Instead, she purchases an immediate annuity. Under a set of life-expectancy tables approved by the government, Sue's life expectancy is 12.05 years. At an assumed interest rate of four percent, the annuity would pay her $875.53 per month for 12 years. When she buys the annuity, Sue will have no assets left. Rather, she will have an income stream of $875.53 for 12 years. Since she has no assets left, all things being equal, she would qualify for Medicaid. Of course, her annuity payment would have to be spent on the nursing home each month. Now say that Sue dies after two years, which is the approximate average length of a nursing home stay. Out of the original $100,000, she would have paid the nursing home $12,012.72 (*i.e.*, $875.53 times 24) over the two years that she was in the nursing home. After Sue's death, the balance of the funds would remain in the annuity, and would be paid to her beneficiaries over the remaining ten years left on the contract. In the unlikely event that Sue lives longer than 12 years, of course, the entire sum would have been paid to the nursing home. If Sue is in good physical health, and there is a reasonable possibility of her actually living for 12 years, then doing a Half-a-Loaf would make more sense than an immediate annuity.

Now let's look at a married couple, Sharon and Mark. It is with the married couple that we see the power of the annuity, since a married couple can use the immediate annuity to shelter 100% of their monetary assets. Recall that the community spouse is permitted to keep half of the monetary assets, up to a certain cap. Say Sharon and Mark have countable assets worth $100,000. Mark, who is in the nursing home, would have to spend down $47,500, and Sharon would be allowed to keep $50,000. Bearing in mind the rule that the spend-down funds can be spent on any-thing, and for either spouse, as long as fair market value is received, Sharon uses the $47,500 in spend-down funds to purchase an immediate annuity for herself. The monthly income from the annuity belongs to her, and, as such, need not be spent on Mark's care. In this way, Mark can immediately qualify for Medicaid assistance, the monthly annuity payments would go to Sharon (who can do with them whatever she wants), and all of the monetary assets have been preserved. The risk in this case is that Sharon would need to go into a nursing home during the life of the annuity. In this event, the annuity payments will have to be spent on her care. As with the single person, the way to avoid this risk would be for Sharon and Mark to do a Half-a-Loaf, and not the annuity. They would save less, but there would be no risk to the funds if Sharon were to need nursing home care. If Sharon and Mark chose to do the annuity, instead of the Half-a-Loaf, the way to minimize the risk that Sharon would need nursing home care during the term of the annuity would be to shorten the term. That is, let's say that Sharon's life expectancy is 10 years. There is nothing to stop her from structuring an annuity contract that pays for less than 10 years. The shorter the term of the annuity, the less the risk that Sharon will get sick and need nursing home care while the annuity is still being paid.

A word of caution about immediate annuities is in order. The rules surrounding immediate annuities are extremely technical, and must be complied with exactly in order for the annuity to work. An immediate annuity is by its very nature irrevocable. Therefore, any error, once made, cannot be corrected. In other words, in order for the annuity to work, it must be done perfectly the first time. There are no second chances with an immediate annuity! If done correctly, which is the job of the Elder Law attorney, the annuity can mean the difference between a life of penury for the surviving spouse and a normal life that he or she deserves.

There are two types of immediate annuities, commercial annuities and private annuities. A commercial annuity is done through an insurance company. The advantage of a commercial annuity is that once it is done, there is nothing further to think about. All you need to do is to collect the check every month. The disadvantage of a commercial annuity is in the interest rate. The way the insurance company makes a profit is to invest the money at a higher rate of interest than is paid to you.

The second kind of immediate annuity is known as a private annuity. With a private annuity, an individual, usually one of your children, takes the place of the insurance company. That is, you transfer the money to a child and enter into a written annuity contract with that child. He then makes the monthly annuity payments to you. The advantage of a private annuity is that the profit that the insurance company would have made with your money is, instead, kept in the family. The disadvantage of a private annuity is that you need to rely on your child or children to make the payments each month.

One more word about annuities is in order. Some unscrupulous insurance salespeople sell deferred annuities to senior citizens, with the false explanation that the annuity is protected from the nursing home, or that all the nursing home can get is the interest and not the principal. Such statements are outright deceptions, and they are made with alarming frequency. Generally, there are two types of annuities. One is the immediate annuity, described above. If done correctly, as we have just seen, an immediate annuity will shelter large amounts of money from the nursing home. The other type of annuity is the deferred annuity. Many senior citizens use deferred annuities for investment purposes. In a deferred annuity, you deposit the money with the insurance company. Much like a bank CD, the insurance company pays interest on the principal of the annuity, and it is designed to grow in value. One major difference between a bank CD and an insurance company deferred annuity, however, is that a deferred annuity can be annuitized, *i.e.*, surrendered to the insurance company and converted to an immediate annuity of the type described above.

It is this feature of a deferred annuity, the ability to quickly annuitize it, or turn it into an income stream, that leads some unscrupulous insurance salespeople to take advantage of senior citizens. That is, they sell a deferred annuity to a senior with the explanation that it is protected from the nursing home, in that the nursing home can only get the interest, and not the principal. This statement, which is repeated to senior citizens time and time again, is false. A deferred annuity is a completely countable asset, offering no nursing home protection at all. The ability to quickly annuitize a deferred annuity, or convert it into an immediate annuity, is actually of no practical value, since virtually any monetary investment can be quickly sold and converted to an immediate annuity at any time.

All this is not to say that deferred annuities are not good investments, and that senior citizens should stay away from them. Rather, a senior who is considering investing in a deferred annuity should do so because he or she thinks it is a good investment, which it very well might be. However, a deferred annuity should never be purchased for nursing home protection, since it affords none at all.

6. Life Care Contracts

Consider this situation. Ralph, age 80, has been diagnosed with early Alzheimer's. At the beginning stages of his disease, he can still cook, keep house and prepare meals, but he can no longer drive or do errands. His daughter, Louise, therefore, starts doing his shopping and his chores. As his Alzheimer's progresses, and he loses the ability to cook and clean, Louise does more and more for him. Eventually, Louise is spending about six to ten hours per week taking care of Ralph. Finally, being the devoted daughter that she is, and wanting to keep her father out of the nursing home for as long as possible, Louise quits her job, moves in with Ralph, and becomes his full-time caregiver.

Recall that a nursing home recipient or spouse can purchase anything he or she wants, as long as fair market value is received. What is to stop Ralph from paying Louise for her efforts? After all, no one is required to work for free, even for their parents. Therefore, Ralph can pay Louise to take care of him, and he can continue to pay her for the rest of his life.

In order to figure out how much he can pay Louise, we consult the same life expectancy tables that are used for immediate annuities. Ralph is 80 years old. His life expectancy is 6.98 years. Say that Louise can document that she spends 50 hours per week taking care of Ralph. If we assume that a reasonable hourly wage for this sort of work is $15 per hour, we can arrive at the salary Louise would earn from Ralph for the rest of his life. Fifty hours per week times $15 per hour times 52 weeks in a year times 6.98 years equals $272,220. Ralph can therefore pay Louise $272,220 in a lump sum, for Louise's agreement to provide care-giving services for the rest of his life.

Of course, it is not as simple as that. In order to withstand the scrutiny of Medicaid, the agreement needs to be in writing, specifying exactly what services Louise is to provide. There needs to be a clause stating what is to happen if Louise, through health or personal reasons of her own, is no longer able to comply with the agreement. Also, Louise would need to know that the funds are taxable to her as income. If Ralph lives longer than the 6.98 years, Louise may have to continue to provide services, though she might be able to claim additional compensation. If Ralph dies before the 6.98 years, Louise is entitled to keep the money. Certainly, a Life Care Contract is an agreement that only a knowledgeable attorney should prepare, because the requirements of both state and federal law need to be complied with.

Chapter 7:

Medicaid Planning for Those Who Have Time to Plan

In the previous chapter, we saw several powerful techniques that can be used for families that are in crisis because they have a loved one who is either in a nursing home or about to go into one. Now, let's look at Medicaid planning for people who are currently healthy, but want to protect their assets should they go into a nursing home in the future. This type of planning can also benefit those people who have received a diagnosis of early Alzheimer's or some other degenerative condition, and who have time to plan their affairs. Such people can do Medicaid planning in advance of a nursing home stay, so that their assets are protected should they have to go into a nursing home in the future.

A. Outright Gifts to the Children

Consider the example of Joe and Nancy. They are in their late sixties. Both are healthy, but like most people, they are concerned that should either one get sick and need nursing home care in the future, they will lose their assets.

They have a modest estate, consisting of a house worth $100,000, CDs worth $75,000 and stock worth $150,000. They have three children, ages 25, 27 and 30. They don't mind using the CDs to pay for a nursing home stay if they need to, but protecting the stock and the house are extremely important to them. Therefore, they put the house and stock into their three children's names.

Joe and Nancy have just made a very serious mistake. By putting the stock and house in their children's names, they have protected these assets from the nursing home, (assuming that they do not need nursing home care within the disqualification period), but they have created a host of serious problems both for themselves and their children, problems that are likely to give them nasty surprises in the future.

First, they have created a tax nightmare for their children, in that they have handed their children a completely unnecessary and avoidable capital gains tax. Federal tax law states that if children (or anyone else, for that matter) inherit assets at death, then, for tax purposes, they inherit the assets at the date of death value. This feature is known as the stepped-up basis. If and when the children later sell the asset, capital gains are based on the sale price less the date of death value.

This rule does not apply, however, to assets gifted during life. Let's look at Joe and Nancy's situation from this tax perspective. The house is worth $100,000, but when Joe and Nancy bought it 40 years ago, they paid only $7,000 for it. Similarly, the stock is worth $150,000, and when they bought it 35 years ago, they paid $30,000. If the children were to have inherited the house at death, and sold it for $100,000, there would have been no capital gains tax. The same rule applies to the stock. This is a result of the stepped-up basis mentioned previously. Because Joe and Nancy gifted the house and stock to the children during life, however, the later capital gains are calculated not on the date of death value, but on the price Joe and Nancy paid for the house and stock years ago. Therefore, when the children sell the house, $93,000 would be subject to capital gains taxes, and when they sell the stock, $120,000 would be subject to capital gains taxes. Had the children inherited these assets at death, capital gains would have been greatly minimized, if not completely eliminated. Certainly, by gifting the house and stock to their children, Joe and Nancy did not do their children any favors.

There is a second tax issue lurking here, though not as serious as the first. Most people know that you can gift $11,000 per year, tax free. In this case, when Joe and Nancy gifted the house and stock, they made a gift of far more than $11,000. Therefore, they were legally required to report this gift to the IRS on a gift tax return, Form 709. Most people do not know this, and fail to file this legally required tax return.

The third problem that Joe and Nancy have created is that the house and stock are subject to their children's liabilities. If one of their children gets divorced or sued, or needs to declare bankruptcy, then Joe and Nancy's house and stock are subject to the children's creditors.

The fourth problem for Joe and Nancy is loss of control. If they want or need to sell the house or stock, they cannot do so, because they don't own them. They would have to go to their children and ask permission to do so. Naturally,

Joe and Nancy have no control over whether their children consent or not.

B. The Medicaid Trust

Since gifting assets to children is so dangerous, it hardly, if ever, should be done as a means of Medicaid Planning. A much better and safer approach than gifting is to prepare what is known as a Special Power of Appointment Irrevocable Trust, also known as a Medicaid Trust. The Medicaid Trust is the pre-eminent method of sheltering assets, since it avoids all of the problems inherent in gifting assets to children.

Here is how the trust works. You transfer to the trust those assets you wish to protect. If those assets generate income, such as interest, dividends or rents, you receive all of the income, just as normal. The trust is able to sell and buy assets, including real estate. So, if you have some stocks in the trust, and if you want to sell them and buy others, you can do so. Or, if you have a CD that matures, you can re-invest the proceeds into whatever kind of asset you want. On your death, the trust passes to the heirs without probate. Of course, it's more complex than that, so let's look at the trust in detail.

First, a Medicaid Trust is subject to a five-year lookback period. The lookback concept is the same as that described earlier, when we spoke about gifting. That is, the value of the assets transferred to the trust is divided by the state's disqualification rate, to determine the waiting period for the trust to shelter assets. For example, if your house is worth $150,000, and the state's disqualification rate is

$4,500, the waiting period would be approximately 33 months. If done correctly, the maximum waiting period would be 60 months. After the waiting period is over, the assets in the trust will be protected from the nursing home. Additionally, the state cannot put a lien against those assets in order to seek recovery for Medicaid benefits paid.

An important feature of the waiting period is that it is not all or nothing meaning that the assets in the trust are protected incrementally. In other words, let's say that you live in a state in which the disqualification rate is $5,000 per month. You have a house worth $250,000 that you transfer into the trust. Simple math tells you that the waiting period for the house to become protected would be 50 months. What happens, however, if you go into a nursing home after 32 months. Is the house lost? Not at all. Over the 32 months since you set up the trust, your equity in the house has been protected, at the rate of $5,000 per month. Therefore, after 32 months, $160,000 worth of house has been protected (32 x $5,000 = $160,000). You are then presented with a choice. First, you can use other assets to pay the nursing home to cover the remaining 18 months of the waiting period, after which time the entire house will be protected. Second, especially if you are unmarried, you can sell the house and protect a large amount of the proceeds. If you sell the house for $250,000, the sum of $160,000 will be protected, and $90,000 will not. Of the $90,000 that is not protected, you can use a technique known as a Half-a-Loaf, described elsewhere in the book, to protect roughly half, or about $45,000. In short, you will have been able to protect $205,000 out of a total of $250,000. That is the power of the Medicaid Trust.

The disadvantage of the Medicaid Trust is that you can no longer have direct access to the principal of the trust. The rule is simple: If you can get the money, the nursing home can get it as well. If you can't get it, the nursing home can't get it. How then can you have access to the funds in the trust? The answer lies in a legal concept known as a Special Power of Appointment. A Special Power of Appointment is the ability to direct where trust assets are distributed, whether during life or after your death. Here is how to use the Special Power of Appointment to obtain principal from the trust, *i.e.*, to take money out of the trust. Say you set up a Medicaid Trust. You are the trustee and you name your three children, for example, as beneficiaries. You have a bank account in the trust name. Now say that you want to use some of this money, maybe to buy a car or take a trip. You go to the bank and have the bank issue a check to one of your children. The child deposits the money in his bank account, and then writes a check for this amount back to you. Remember, you can gift $11,000 per person per year without any tax reporting, and your children can do likewise. Thus, up to $11,000 per year can go to each child and back to you, without any tax consequences. A married couple can give $11,000 per spouse, or $22,000. So, if you are married, and have three children, you can transfer $66,000 per year this way (i.e., $11,000 per spouse times two, times three children).

How do you guarantee that your children will gift the money back? Therein lies the magic of the Special Power of Appointment. Under the Special Power of Appointment, which is a provision contained in the trust, you are allowed to change the beneficiaries of the Trust. In effect, you can disinherit your children from the trust, and you make sure that they know it. If you give a child money from the trust, and he does not return it to you, you can "exercise" the Special Power of Appointment to make sure that this child never receives any additional money from the trust. Faced with the prospect of being disinherited, the children, of course, will cooperate and return the money.

The Medicaid Trust is irrevocable. There are a great many misconceptions about irrevocable trusts, as follows:

1. Many people think that you need an independent trustee. While this is true of some irrevocable trusts, it is not true of the Medicaid Trust. With the Medicaid Trust, you can be your own trustee. As such, you can continue to manage your own investments, and you are not answerable to anyone.

2. If you put your house into a Medicaid Trust, you can still sell it. Selling a house through a trust is actually quite easy. The trust, with you in control as trustee, sells the house. The buyer, instead of making out his check to you personally, makes it payable to the trust. You deposit the check into a bank account in the name of the trust, and use that money to buy your next house, in the trust name. If you choose not to buy another house, or if you buy a less expensive house, you keep any unused money in an account in the trust name.

3. There are absolutely no income tax disadvantages to a Medicaid Trust. That is, you can put your house into the trust, as many people do, and still keep the capital gains tax exclusion. In other words, if you sell

your house, the law allows a capital gains exclusion of up to $250,000 for a single person, and up to $500,000 for a married couple. If your house is in the Medicaid Trust, you do not lose these valuable tax breaks. Similarly, any appreciated assets in the trust, such as real estate or stock, still get the benefit of the stepped-up tax basis on death.

4. The Medicaid Trust is not subject to any tax reporting. In other words, while the Medicaid authorities do not view the trust as being your asset (which is why it is protected from the nursing home), the IRS still views the trust as yours. For this reason, you still file your normal tax returns, and the trust is not required to file at all.

Everyone uses the Medicaid Trust differently. Some people use it to protect their house only, while others use it to protect some of their liquid assets, such as stocks or CDs. Let's look at the house. The Medicaid Trust is ideal to protect your house from a long-term nursing home stay. Say your house is worth $150,000, and the disqualification rate is $4,500 per month. If you deed your house into the Medicaid Trust, it will be protected after 33 months. Further, since a house is not liquid, like money, the children have no involvement at all with the house. You are free to sell the house through the trust if you want to, and buy another one in the trust. If you do, the new house will be protected as well. Since the trust is selling the house, and the trust is buying another one, the children have no involvement in this process.

With regard to liquid assets, many senior citizens have a sum of money that they consider to be their nest egg, *i.e.*, money that they are not using on a daily basis, but that they are holding for their security. Perhaps this nest egg is a CD that has not been touched for many years, or some stock that they received years ago, as part of their salary. Such funds are ideal for placement into the Medicaid Trust. The fact that the funds can only be accessed through the children is not a drawback, since these are funds that are not generally used anyway. Further, after the waiting period is over, you can have the peace of mind of knowing that these assets are protected from the nursing home.

The federal law which relates to Medicaid Trusts is known as OBRA '93. Since the intent of OBRA '93 was to tighten up on the Medicaid rules, some attorneys took the position that these Medicaid trusts would no longer be effective. On December 23, 1993, however, the Health Care Finance Agency, which at that time was the federal department that administers the Medicaid program, dispelled this fear by issuing an interpretation of the relevant portion of OBRA '93 to state that, after the appropriate waiting period, (*i.e.,* the value of the trust divided by the state's disqualification rate) the assets in the trust would be protected from long-term care. However, if you are considering such a trust, it is absolutely essential that you work with an Elder Law attorney who is current on the latest laws. This is because some states, such as Connecticut, have significant restrictions on the use of such trusts.

C. The Revocable Trust with Medicaid Triggers

Despite the fact that the Medicaid Trust has a proven track record of protecting assets, it is not for everyone. Some people do not want to do anything having the label irrevocable.

Others do not want their children to have any involvement with their affairs. For these persons, there is an alternative. One of the predominant Medicaid Planning tools has become, in recent years, the Revocable Trust with Medicaid Triggers. The beauty of the Revocable Trust with Medicaid Triggers is that it can allow your family to implement Medicaid Planning for you in the future, if, due to illness or incapacity, you are no longer able to do so on your own. As we saw in an earlier chapter, a Revocable Trust is a legal document that serves the same purpose as a will, but which avoids probate at death. However, the Revocable Trust goes beyond mere probate avoidance, in that it also has provisions for a successor trustee, usually one of the children, to manage the trust in the event you become incompetent. In this way, the trust (in conjunction with the Durable Power of Attorney) avoids guardianship proceedings.

What are Medicaid Triggers, and how can they help shelter assets from the nursing home? Another chapter discussed several Medicaid Planning techniques which can be used if your loved one needs long-term care. For example, there is the immediate annuity, Half-a-Loaf and Life-Care Contract. In earlier parts of the book, we have explored other possibilities, such as converting countable assets into non-countable ones, including prepaid funerals, home improvements, and an automobile. Another example is the caretaker child exception to the transfer-of-asset rules, which allows a house to be deeded to a child who has kept you out of the nursing home for two years. What do all of these techniques have in common? They require that you take action: signing a deed, signing a contract, or buying something. If you are incompetent or incapacitated, then, by definition, you would not be able to do any of these things.

Why can't your Successor Trustee simply do them for you? The answer is that a Successor Trustee does not have blanket authority to do anything on your behalf. Rather, the Successor Trustee can only do those things that the Trust authorizes him to do. That is why any well-written trust will have detailed provisions specifying the powers of the trustee. If you become incompetent and go into the nursing home, and if your Successor Trustee tries to do a Half-a-Loaf, or enter into a Life-Care Contract, and if such powers are not included within the authority granted by the Trust, then chances are the state Medicaid authorities will disallow what he did.

The Medicaid Triggers address this problem. Medicaid Triggers are detailed provisions that allow your trustee to do the following things, among others:

1. Represent you before the state Medicaid authorities, both in applying for benefits and in claiming a fair hearing;
2. Apply for a Resource Assessment;
3. Secure the Minimum Monthly Maintenance Needs Allowance;
4. Convert countable assets into non-countable ones;
5. Employ the caretaker child exception;
6. Rent your house, to make the house non-countable;
7. Do a Half-a-Loaf;
8. Enter into a commercial or private annuity;
9. Enter into a Life Care Contract;
10. Enter into a Self-Canceling Installment Note; and
11. Use whatever other techniques Congress may create in the future.

We call these provisions Medicaid Triggers because the Successor Trustee's ability to do them is triggered by your entry into the nursing home. The Triggers are akin to a menu in a restaurant. They contain all of the possible techniques from which to choose, even though only one or two may be relevant to your situation.

When you create a Revocable Trust with Medicaid Triggers, it is also essential that you insert the Triggers into the Durable Power of Attorney that is usually done with the Trust. The reason is that there are certain assets, such as IRAs, 401(k)s and other tax-deferred retirement accounts that cannot be put into the name of the trust. Additionally, you may have forgotten to put all of your other assets into the trust name. Therefore, the Successor Trustee of the Trust does not have the ability to do any Medicaid Planning with these assets, since they are not a part of the Trust. If, however, the Durable Power of Attorney contains the Triggers, then the Attorney-in-Fact would be able to shelter these assets, as well.

Every Revocable Trust should have Medicaid Triggers, even if the grantor of the trust (*i.e.*, the person who sets it up) is not concerned about nursing homes. Adding the Triggers to a trust has no disadvantage whatsoever; rather, the Triggers set the stage, so to speak, for your Successor Trustee to engage in Medicaid Planning should the need arise later on.

Chapter 8:

Sheltering the House with Medicaid Planning

I n many cases, the family home is not only the most valuable asset, but it is the one to which the most emotion is attached. People spend 30 years paying off a mortgage and pay thousands of dollars in property taxes. They raise their children in the family home, plant trees, bury beloved pets in the backyard, and host graduation parties and wedding receptions there. Normally placid people, who might be able to bear spending their life savings on the nursing home, become enraged at the thought of the house, "Going to the state." Of anything, the house is the one asset that people want most to pass down to their children. When it comes to a house on a lake or at the beach, emotions run even stronger. Probably because home ownership is so basic a value to our society, Medicaid has special rules concerning the house.

A. Estate Recovery

As stated above, the house is not a countable asset as long as both spouses are alive and the community spouse is living in the house. In this case, the house is not subject to claim by the state, and need not be sold to pay for nursing home care of the institutionalized spouse. Elizabeth can be in the nursing home on Medicaid for two years and pass away. Her husband, Luke, can live on another 25 years, and the state will not touch the house during Luke's life. Things become drastically different, however, when Luke dies. Under OBRA '93, which we visited in the last chapter when we discussed Medicaid Trusts, states are required to enact so-called estate recovery programs. Estate recovery means that the state puts a claim on the estate of the surviving spouse of a Medicaid recipient. (The state also has a claim against the estate of an unmarried Medicaid recipient. However, since an unmarried Medicaid recipient can own no more than $2,500 or so worth of countable assets, estate recovery usually is not a major issue in the case of an unmarried person.) In this way, the state seeks to recover, or claim repayment, of its Medicaid costs, prior to any inheritance going to the children.

Many people view estate recovery as the most offensive feature of the Medicaid program. Estate recovery has been called a death tax on the middle class and working poor. First, it represents double taxation. That is, we pay taxes during our life to fund government programs, including Medicaid. Then, after death, the government takes the family's assets a second time, to reimburse itself for the Medicaid benefits that our tax dollars paid for in the first place. Imagine a law that said that if you become unemployed and collect unemployment compensation, you must repay the state from your salary after you land a new job. Estate recovery is really the same thing. Second, estate recovery robs people of one of the most fundamental of human desires, that of leaving at least a small inheritance to their children and grandchildren. After the tragedy of going into a nursing home in the first place, and spending virtually all of your money to pay for it, estate recovery is the final indignity.

Let's go back to Luke and Elizabeth, our married couple. Elizabeth goes into the nursing home, and the couple pays privately until their countable assets are below the allowed amount. Elizabeth then qualifies for Medicaid. Say she is a Medicaid recipient for two years, and during those two years, the state pays the nursing home $4,000 per month, or $96,000 in total. Elizabeth then dies. During Luke's life, the state is prohibited from making any claims against him for reimbursement for Elizabeth's care. At Luke's death, however, the state is required to make a claim against his estate to recover the amount spent on Elizabeth's nursing home care. Say at his death, Luke still owns the house, which is worth $150,000. That is his only asset. When Luke's estate is being settled, the state will force the sale of the house. After the house is sold, the state will be repaid its $96,000 claim, and the balance will go to the heirs. If the house is only worth $85,000, then the state will get the entire proceeds, and the heirs will get nothing. In some states, estate recovery is limited only to the assets going through probate, so if the house is placed into a Revocable Trust, which avoids probate, the state's claim is avoided, and the house will be saved. Under federal law, though, states have the option of making claims against living trusts or other devices which avoid probate. Some states do so, and others do not, but the national trend is to be more aggressive in this direction.

B. *Allowable Transfers of the House*

There are some federal laws which allow the transfer (*i.e.*, gifting) of the house to certain favored individuals. As we saw in an earlier chapter, the law authorizes the transfer of a house to a spouse, a blind child, a child with permanent and total disability, a child under 21 or a sibling with an equity interest in the house who has lived there for over a year. A house can also be transferred to a child who has lived in the home, and who has provided services to the parent, and kept the parent out of the nursing home for at least two years.

C. *Outright Gift of the House to Children*

Of course, you can make an outright gift of your house to your children simply by putting the deed in their names. Doing this is easy, and it can be done at minimal cost. However, putting your house in your children's names is the worst mistake that you can make when it comes to Medicaid planning. There are three reasons why gifting the house to children is almost never appropriate:

Liability-If you put your house in your children's names, you make it subject to their liabilities: if they get sued, you get sued. The reason is simple. The house now belongs to your children and not you. A creditor of your child could put an attachment on your house, and you can actually lose your house if your child files for bankruptcy. If your child gets divorced, you can find that your house becomes part of his property settlement.

Loss of Control – Consider the example of Father and Daughter. Father wants to protect his house from the nursing home, so he puts the house into Daughter's name. Daughter is a "good kid," and is completely trustworthy, Dad reasons, so he is not worried about liability problems. Daughter is single, but she is seeing someone, Harold, that Father has very bad feelings about. Harold has no job, does not speak in full sentences, and has a shaved head with a small tattoo of the Confederate flag. One day, Daughter comes home elated, with the news that, "Harold has just asked me to marry him, and I said yes!" Of course Father's entreaties to get Daughter to reconsider fall on deaf ears, and they get married. Some time thereafter, Daughter gets very sick with a fatal disease, and dies before Father. Daughter had the foresight to make a will before she died, leaving everything she owned, including Father's house, to Harold. Harold is now Father's landlord! Enough said.

Taxes – In many cases, a gift of the house to the children is actually a gift to the IRS. Here is why. Say you bought your house in 1962, for $20,000. At your death it is worth $220,000. If your children inherit the house when you die, then, for tax purposes, they inherit it for the $220,000 value. If they sell it for that value, they pay no capital gains taxes. Now say that you make a gift of the house to the children during your life. If you do that, you change the tax rules. The children no longer inherit the house for the $220,000 it is worth at your death, but instead they inherit it for the $20,000 you paid in 1962. If they sell it for $220,000, then all of the growth, or $200,000 is subject to capital gains taxes. In reality, then, you have made a voluntary contribution to the IRS, because you have created an unnecessary tax.

As can be seen, an outright gift of the house to the children is the worst way of protecting it, since it exposes the house to more liabilities and problems than protections.

D. *Life Estate Deeds*

Another alternative is to deed the house to the children subject to a "retained life estate." This is called a life estate deed. A life estate is the right of a person, called "the grantor," to live in the house for the duration of his life. In other words, if Mother deeds the house to Son subject to a life estate, title will be in Son's name, but Mother can continue to live in the house, rent free, until she passes away.

Medicaid law has strict regulations concerning life estate deeds. When a parent transfers a deed to child (or anyone else) subject to a life estate, he is actually only transferring what is known as a future interest, *i.e.*, the right to ownership of the house in the future, after the parent dies. This is because during the parent's lifetime, the parent continues to live in the house. The children only have the right to occupancy at an indeterminate time in the future. Thus, it should be clear that when the parent deeds a house to the children subject to a life estate, the parent transfers partial ownership rights, and retains partial ownership rights. Remember that any time an asset is transferred within 36 months of a Medicaid application, the state will assess a Medicaid penalty, which is equal to the value of the asset transferred divided by the state's disqualification rate. How do you value the partial ownership rights transferred with a life estate deed? The federal government has issued a table which assigns a value to a life estate. The value changes with age, since the older a person gets, the shorter his life expectancy. Obviously, a life estate retained by a 95-year old is worth less than one retained by a 70-year old, because the 70-year old is expected to live longer than the 95-year old. How do we determine this value? Say that Wilfred, age 65, transfers his house to his son, Michael. The house is worth $100,000. Under the government tables, the value of Wilfred's life estate is $67,970, and the value of the future interest given to Michael would be $32,030. Since Wilfred started with an asset worth $100,000, and retained a life estate worth $67,970, he would be deemed to have gifted an asset worth $32,030. In a state with a disqualification rate of $4,500 per month, the disqualification period on account of this gift would be approximately seven months.

Will the value of a life estate be subject to estate recovery after the parent has died? This is an open question, handled differently in each state. As we saw earlier, federal law gives the states the option of seeking estate recovery from the value of a life estate after the Medicaid recipient has died. Therefore, the answer is different in each state. Assuming that the state does seek recovery, what is the value of a life estate of someone who has died? Is it zero, since a dead person has no life expectancy, or is it the full value of the life estate when given, or is it the value of the life estate based on the person's age when he or she died? As yet, neither the courts nor the Medicaid authorities have definitively answered these questions.

What happens if the property subject to a life estate is sold during the parent's lifetime? Consider the above example. A few years after Wilfred deeds the house to Michael subject to the life estate, Wilfred goes into the nursing home, and eventually ends up on Medicaid. The house is vacant, and Michael wants to sell it. Doing so, however, might not be a good idea. Remember the value of the life estate, $67,970 in this example. If the house is sold during Wilfred's lifetime, then he will be entitled to $67,970 worth of the proceeds, all of which will be a countable asset, and will either have to be spent on the nursing home or repaid to the state as reimbursement for Medicaid benefits paid. It would be a much better idea for Michael to rent out the house during his father's lifetime, and then sell it after his father has died, when the life estate has been extinguished.

One advantage of the Life Estate Deed is that only the children's future interest is subject to attachment by their creditors. That is, if the children get sued or divorced, the only interest in the house that they really own is the right to possess the house in the future. Therefore, a creditor can only attach that future interest. A disadvantage of a Life Estate Deed, however, is loss of control. If a parent wants to sell the house during his lifetime, then he would have to get the children's permission to do so. Obviously, the parent has no control over whether or not the children would consent to a sale. If the children do consent to the sale, then IRS regulations state that they are entitled to a part of the purchase price, and they would be liable for capital gains taxes on their share. Say that the children pay the taxes, and then turn over the proceeds to the parent. If these proceeds exceed $11,000, then there might be gift tax consequences for the children. All things considered, a transfer of the house subject to a life estate is better than an outright deed without a life estate, but not by much.

E. Self-Canceling Installment Note

Another planning option with the home is a sale to the children, with a "Self-Canceling Installment Note" (SCIN). A SCIN is a promissory note that is canceled, or forgiven, on the death of the parent-seller. For example, Henry sells his house to his daughter, Louise, for a note calling for payments of $15,000 per year for 10 years, or $1,250 per month. Henry goes into the nursing home, and Louise is making the payments. After two years, Henry dies. Louise has paid $30,000 (*i.e.,* $1,250 per month for 24 months). The note is canceled when Henry dies, and Louise makes no more payments. Thus, she has paid $30,000 for a house worth $150,000.

Since Louise gave Henry a legitimate promissory note for full value when she bought the house, there is no Medicaid disqualification period. Additionally, the payments can be structured to suit Louise's financial circumstances. The balance due on the note at Henry's death is not subject to estate recovery, because, at his death, there is no balance due.

Obviously, a competent attorney must be consulted in order to prepare the SCIN. Additionally, a CPA should be consulted, since the tax consequences of the SCIN are extremely complex and must be assessed as part of the transaction.

F. Special Power of Appointment Deed

Another method of protecting the house is a deed to the children subject to a Special Power of Appointment (SPA Deed). We have already met the Special Power of

Appointment when we discussed the Medicaid Trust. The SPA Deed protects the house from long-term care and estate recovery, while allowing the parent to have control over the house. Here is how a SPA Deed works. Say that Tom has three children, Amanda, Joanne and Stephen. Tom deeds the house to all three, subject however, to his right to appoint, or re-direct ownership, at any time and in any proportion, to Amanda, Joanne, Stephen, or their children. In other words, Tom has given the house to the three children, but retains the right to change the ownership later on. SPA Deeds are difficult to understand, because they involve deeding the house to someone, and then being able to take it away and give it to someone else. This right to give the house to someone else, however, is extremely valuable. That is, after the Medicaid disqualification period on account of the gift has ended, the property is protected from the nursing home, but is still subject to Tom's control. That is, the SPA allows Tom to divest Amanda, Joanne and Stephen of ownership, either in full or in part. For this reason, on fear of losing the property, the three children will do what their father wants them to do.

G. Conversion of the House to Rental Property

Another alternative would be to convert the house to rental property. Say that Ralph, a widower, goes into the nursing home. Ralph's only asset is his home. Medicaid law says that a rental property is not a countable asset, as long as the rentals cover the costs (property taxes, insurance and maintenance). Therefore, Ralph's daughter, acting as Attorney-in-Fact, rents the house to a third party, and turns over the net rentals to Ralph. Ralph pays the net rentals to the nursing home, along with the rest of his income. Since the house is now rental property, it is not countable, and does not have to be sold in order for Ralph to receive Medicaid benefits. The problem, however, is that the house would be subject to estate recovery on Ralph's death. To avoid this result, Ralph can deed the rented house to his daughter, subject to a life estate. (Ralph's retention of a life estate also means that he is still entitled to receive the net rents.) Doing so would not violate the transfer-of-asset rules, because there is no Medicaid penalty for transfer of a non-countable asset. Would this strategy work? It depends on how aggressive the state Medicaid authorities are. Under the law, there is no reason why this would not work. However, this is so aggressive a technique that it is not frequently done.

H. Special Power of Appointment Trust

The final method of protecting the house is to put it into a Special Power of Appointment Medicaid Trust, discussed in detail in an earlier chapter. The trust avoids the disadvantages inherent in an outright gift to the children, in several respects. First, the house is not subject to the children's liabilities, since it is not in their name. Additionally, recall the Special Power of Appointment, which allows you to change the beneficiaries. If one of your children should get sued or divorced, and you want to protect his share from his creditors, you can simply exercise the Special Power of Appointment to shift his share to your other children. Second, there are no loss of control problems, since you are the trustee of the trust. The children avoid the capital gains taxes on death, since they inherit the house for its date of death value. Finally, the house avoids probate on your death.

Chapter 9:

Special Issues Posed by Second Marriages

Love is lovelier, the second time around. Just as wonderful, with both feet on the ground. It's that second time you hear your love song sung. Makes you think, perhaps, that love, like youth, is wasted on the young.

> From, "The Second Time Around," Lyrics by Sammy Cahn and Jimmy Van Heusen, made famous by Bing Crosby in the movie, *High Time* (1960)

As the old Bing Crosby standard says, September romances can indeed be more satisfying the "second time around." This must be true, judging from the high rate at which our senior clients get married for the second time. Very often, marrying for a second time in retirement years makes people seem more energetic, vibrant, and alive. It gives them a fresh outlook on life, and can even, it seems, make them live longer.

Yet what can be a blessing to most seniors can quickly become a curse if one of them enters a nursing home. Take the example of Harold and Betty, both in their eighties, married for a second time, and both with grown children from their first marriages. Here are their assets:

Harold		Betty	
House	$250,000	Beach house	$300,000
CDs	100,000	CDs	25,000
Savings	10,000	Savings	30,000

About six years ago, Betty was diagnosed with Alzheimer's disease and Harold has been taking care of her at home since that time. Betty's condition has lately become much worse, however, and Harold's doctor told him that his own health would begin to suffer unless Betty goes into a nursing home.

Although Harold owns the house, he and Betty moved out a year ago. Harold enjoys doing yard work and the odd jobs necessary to maintain a house. He is still physically active and healthy, and things like mowing the lawn, painting, gardening and shoveling snow get him fresh air and exercise. As he puts it, "Puttering around the house keeps me young." Unfortunately, however, Betty's condition has become such that she has started to require constant care, and Harold no longer has enough time to do the chores that he so much likes to do. Therefore, they moved out of the house a year ago and signed a two-year lease on an apartment. Harold has not sold the house, however, because it has come down from his first wife's side of the family, and he wants his children to inherit it when he passes away.

Before getting married, Harold and Betty signed a premarital agreement, which essentially says that Harold's assets go to his two children on his death, and Betty's assets go to her two children. The agreement also says that Harold and Betty are going to keep their assets separate, and that each is not going to be responsible for the other's debts and obligations. Betty's children, in particular, are concerned about the beach house, which they all love, and which has increased in value dramatically over the years. Much of Harold's money, including the house, was inherited from his first wife's side of the family, and Harold's children do not want to see their father lose these assets for the care of Betty, who is largely a stranger to them.

Harold, accompanied by his two children, goes to see an Elder Law attorney, and asks for the attorney's help in qualifying Betty for Medicaid as soon as possible. He gives the attorney a copy of a durable power of attorney that Betty signed, naming him as her attorney-in-fact. What issues are presented here? Let's see what would happen if Harold were to do nothing. Although Harold is worried about loss of his assets, he is not overly concerned. He and Betty paid a reputable lawyer good money to write a premarital agreement, which says that their assets and debts are separate. The lawyer assured them that the premarital agreement was valid and enforceable under the laws of their state. Well, Harold is in for a very rude surprise. While a premarital agreement is generally enforceable as to inheritance, divorce and creditor issues, it is decidedly **not** enforceable when it comes to nursing homes and Medicaid. That is, a premarital agreement is valid and enforceable because it is made under the authority of state law. Medicaid, as we have seen in earlier chapters, is based on federal law, and *federal law supercedes any contrary* *state law.* Therefore, the Elder Law attorney advises Harold, much to Harold's astonishment, that the premarital agreement might as well not even exist: for Medicaid purposes, it has no force at all. This is the first lesson that people who marry later in life need to know. Premarital agreement or not, and whether they keep their assets separate or not, when the couple says, "I do," for Medicaid purposes, they have consented to make their assets available to the other one's nursing home costs. For the couple involved in the second marriage, then, some form of asset protection is *essential.* Generally speaking, either the Medicaid Trust or, at the very least, the Revocable Trust with Medicaid Triggers, should be seriously considered.

Let's get back to Harold. The attorney gives Harold and his children a minute to get over their shock, and then presents the following rather grim analysis: Both Harold's house and Betty's house are countable assets. That is, the rule that the community spouse's house is non-countable only applies if the house is used as his or her homestead. Recall that while Harold owns the house, he does not live in it. Therefore, it loses its non-countable status, and becomes fully countable. Betty's beach house is also countable, for the same reason. (Note that if Harold lived in his house, it would not be countable, while Betty's house would be countable in any event, since there is no protection for second houses.) Therefore, the attorney explains, Harold is allowed to keep the first $89,000 worth of assets, Betty can keep $2,500 worth of assets, and the rest of the assets need to be spent down before Betty is eligible for Medicaid. The fact that Harold's house and most of his money were inherited from his first wife is completely irrelevant.

After giving Harold and his children this bad news, the Elder Law attorney goes on to discuss possible solutions. If Harold wants to qualify Betty for Medicaid immediately, then he can keep his $89,000, sell his house, have Betty sell her house, and put the proceeds into an immediate annuity (either a commercial annuity with an insurance company, or a private annuity, with the children) from which he will derive the income. Assuming that the annuity is set up to comply with the legal requirements we have seen in another chapter, then Betty will qualify for Medicaid.

What are the issues raised by this solution? First, Harold will need to sell the house that he always wanted his children to inherit, and he will forever lose any chance of doing the yard work and tinkering that he loves. Betty's children will also lose the beach house. Worse, the proceeds of the sale of Betty's beach house, as well as her savings and CDs, will, through the annuity, be payable to Harold; this result will completely violate their intention, as expressed in the premarital agreement, of keeping their assets separate! The inheritance that Betty intended for her children will go to Harold through the annuity, and, when he dies, this money will go to Harold's children. Betty's children, the attorney explains, are the beneficiaries of the premarital agreement. If Harold goes the annuity route, Betty's children might even be able to sue Harold, or Harold's children, for breach of the premarital agreement. Harold, like most senior citizens, is scrupulously honest, and has a rock-solid belief in honoring his commitments. Thus, he would not even consider taking Betty's money, and the thought of being sued by her children sends chills down his spine.

At this point, the Elder Law attorney presents another piece of information, that of "conflict of interest." That, is, exactly whom does the attorney represent? Attorneys are bound by strict rules of ethics, including rules as to conflicts of interest. That is, contrary to what most people think, if parties to a matter have differing legal interests, (*i.e.*, if a legal solution will benefit one party and will harm another), then an attorney can only represent one person. In this case, the annuity will benefit Harold, but will harm Betty and/or Betty's children. Thus, in situations such as presented by Harold and Betty, the attorney cannot represent the family unit, but, rather, can represent only Betty or Harold. If the attorney represents Harold, then a second, independent attorney will need to be brought in to represent Betty, and vice versa.

The Elder Law attorney then goes on to present more options. Another possible solution is a so-called "Medicaid Divorce." Recall that there is no Medicaid penalty (or disqualification) for transfers of assets between spouses. Thus, Harold files for divorce. During the course of the divorce proceedings, but while Betty and Harold are still married, Betty transfers all of her assets to Harold, leaving her destitute. Then, they formalize this arrangement in a divorce stipulation, which the court approves. Betty is qualified for Medicaid, since she has no assets. After Medicaid has been approved, Harold transfers the assets that were formerly Betty's to her children.

What are the problems and conflict of interest issues here? First, the idea of divorce is abhorrent to Harold, as it would be to most people of his generation. To Harold, marriage is a life long commitment, and, if he divorced Betty, especially in her sick and vulnerable condition, he would not be able to look himself in the mirror each day. Getting beyond Harold's emotional commitment to Betty and distaste of divorce, a divorce would put Harold in a very precarious legal condition. That is, say that he did divorce Betty, and then honored his commitment to turn over Betty's property to her children. Legally, as a result of the divorce stipulation, Betty's assets belong to Harold. If he were to turn those assets over to Betty's children, the law would look at that as a gift. What would happen, then, if Harold were to get sick, and need nursing home care himself, during the three-year Medicaid lookback period after having made the gift to Betty's children? He would be disqualified for Medicaid, since he made a gift of valuable assets. He will have sacrificed his own assets as a result of having protected Betty's children.

For ethical reasons, many attorneys would refuse to represent Harold in a Medicaid Divorce. That is, most states have enacted so-called "no fault" divorce statutes. Generally, these statutes require that the party suing for divorce testify in court that the marriage has broken down irretrievably, or that the spouses have irreconcilable differences. Say Harold were to testify in this manner. Would he be telling the truth when on the witness stand? He still loves Betty, and it breaks his heart that she has to go into a nursing home. If he testifies that his marriage has broken down irretrievably, when in fact he still loves Betty and wishes that she could come home, isn't he committing perjury? Isn't the real reason for the divorce that he wants to shelter assets, and that, in fact, his marriage has not broken down? If Betty were competent, and heard Harold testifying under oath that their marriage had broken down, wouldn't she be devastated?

On the other hand, attorneys who do not have a problem with Medicaid Divorces make this argument: A marriage, by definition, involves two people who have made a commitment to each other, and who live a life together. Where one spouse has lost his or her mental competency due to Alzheimer's he or she no longer has the mental or physical capacity to be a partner in a marriage. If that spouse, who has no capacity to be a marriage partner, then has to go into a nursing home permanently, there really is no marriage left, is there? A marriage, in any meaningful sense, has been made impossible by the circumstances. When viewed in this light, isn't it true that the marriage has indeed broken down irretrievably? Of course, there is no one correct answer to this ethical dilemma, and each attorney needs to answer this question for him or herself.

Finally, the Elder Law Attorney presents a third option. Harold breaks his lease and moves back into his house. Any damages payable to the landlord as a result of Harold's breach of the lease are paid from Betty's funds, as part of the Medicaid spenddown. Betty pays for the nursing home until her funds are exhausted, leaving Harold with his house and $110,000 in the bank. Harold keeps his $89,000, and puts $21,000 into an annuity on himself. Betty qualifies for Medicaid, and Harold keeps his assets. The "losers," in this scenario are Betty and her children, but at least this is in keeping with the parties' understanding under the premarital agreement. Of course, the Elder Law attorney still has the same conflict of interest issue, so independent counsel would have to represent Betty's side of the family.

There is another issue that affects seniors in this position. In most cases, the children of seniors involved in second marriages are strangers to one another. Very often, they live in different states, they only met at the wedding, and, at best, they see each other once a year at Christmas or Thanksgiving. But for the fact that their parents are married, they have nothing in common with each other. As the case of Harold and Betty illustrates, these children have very different interests from each other, and, more often than not, what benefits one side of the family harms the other. A great deal of resentment and hostility can build up if a child's expected inheritance is lost to pay for the nursing home care of someone who is very nearly a stranger.

Recall from an earlier chapter that a requirement of getting Medicaid for a married couple is a Resource Assessment. The Resource Assessment is a detailed list of all of the assets of both spouses as of the date the ill spouse is institutionalized. Let's go back to our Harold and Betty example, but let's change the facts somewhat. Say that Harold, while not incompetent, no longer has any interest in managing his finances. Say that, like many seniors, he has turned over management of his finances to his children. Prior to Betty getting Medicaid, she has to do a Resource Assessment. She needs the cooperation of Harold's children, doesn't she? Harold's children are no friend of Betty at this point, and they do not cooperate in turning over Harold's records to the Medicaid agency. Therefore, the Resource Assessment cannot get done, and Betty cannot get the Medicaid benefits that she needs. Obviously, we have quite a problem, and, unfortunately, a problem which is not that infrequent.

In writing this chapter, it was not our intention to discourage seniors from getting married later in life. It was our intention, however, to alert seniors to the pitfalls and "traps for the unwary" that can await them if one of them gets sick and needs nursing home care later on. How can seniors thinking about getting married protect themselves and their children? When contemplating marriage, a visit to an Elder Law attorney is essential, as it can prevent the very real "parade of horribles" that we have recited above.

First, a premarital agreement is a must. As we have seen, such an agreement will have no effect whatsoever on sheltering assets from the nursing home. However, a premarital agreement can deal with other important issues, such as inheritance rights, separate ownership of assets, and property settlements in the event of divorce. Of course, such an agreement isn't very romantic, but, as the song with which we opened this chapter states, second love is " Just as wonderful [but] with both feet on the ground." Senior Citizens, having had a whole lifetime of experience, know that marriage, in addition to being about love, has serious financial overtones, as well. A premarital agreement deals with those unpleasant, but necessary, financial issues.

Second, to avoid the Harold and Betty situation, people contemplating second marriages can put in place the Medicaid Trust that we visited in an earlier chapter. This trust is an excellent way of protecting both monetary assets and real estate. You can draw the income from the assets and direct how the assets are invested. Using the children as intermediaries, as explained earlier, you can have access to the principal of the trust. You can live in the house, and can sell it, if you want to do so. After the relevant waiting period for the trust has expired, the trust assets will be safe. In the second marriage context, the Medicaid Trust can be crucial. Say that Betty and Harold had each established such a trust at the time of their marriage. By the time that Betty had to go into a nursing home, both sets of assets would have been protected. Betty would have qualified for Medicaid immediately, and neither Betty nor Harold would have lost anything. Just as significantly, there would have been no conflict of interest issues, relations between their children would have remained friendly, and they would not have had to go through any of the gyrations suggested by the Elder Law attorney. For these reasons, anyone contemplating a second marriage should consider such a trust as a standard operating procedure.

Chapter 10:

How to Choose an Elder Law Attorney

Whena you are faced with a loved one having a diagnosis of a serious illness, or worse, being required to enter a nursing home, you will undoubtedly feel stressed and overwhelmed. You will feel guilty at having had to place your loved one in a nursing home. If you have cared for your loved one at home, you will be exhausted, physically and emotionally. You will have been dealing with doctors, nurses, hospitals, case managers and social workers, all of whom seem to be speaking a strange language, with new words and terms. You will also be terrified at the prospect of losing your home and life savings.

With all of this going on, the job of locating and working with the proper attorney can seem like one more stress for which you need to somehow muster the energy. The search is not made any easier by the fact that Elder Law attorneys are a very small minority of the attorney population, and there may not be one in your area. Although the search will be more difficult than looking for an attorney to do something routine such as a house closing or a simple will, it is absolutely crucial that you seek proper representation. Due to the technicalities and complexities of Medicaid law, some of which we have seen in this book, most lawyers are not equipped to deal with Medicaid issues. Any extra time or travel you need to put in to find the proper attorney will be well worth it for you.

The first place to start the search will likely be with your family attorney, or an attorney with whom you have dealt in the past. For the reasons stated above, it is unlikely that he will have had much experience with Elder Law. However, he can very likely make you a referral, or at least point you in the right direction. Similarly, your accountant or financial advisor might have some referrals. An excellent source for referrals is The National Academy of Elder Law Attorneys (NAELA), 1604 Country Club Road, Tucson, Arizona 85719, 520-881-4005, www.naela.org. NAELA is a nationwide organization of Elder Law attorneys, all of whom practice Medicaid law. While not all Elder Law attorneys are members of NAELA, all NAELA members are Elder Law attorneys. NAELA can provide you with a directory of its members, and can also send you a brochure entitled, "Questions and Answers When Looking for an Elder Law Attorney." Just send a stamped, self-addressed envelope to the above address.

When you have gotten a referral, you will need to sit down with the attorney for an initial conference. Some attorneys might provide a free initial conference, and others might charge a modest fee. Your goal at the initial interview will be to determine if this is the right attorney for you. You have every right to know, and should find out, how many cases such as yours this attorney has handled, and what his success rate has been. You do not want him learning on your case! You should find out what professional organizations he belongs to, such as NAELA, or the Elder Law section of his state bar association. You should also find out what the fees will be. There are two ways that Elder Law attorneys charge, either by the hour or a flat fee.

Hourly billing is straightforward, though among Elder Law attorneys, it is rare. You will probably find that most Elder Law attorneys charge flat fees, that is, a set fee for the project. You might be taken aback at the size of the fee; however, you need to understand that you are not paying for the attorney's time. Rather, you are paying for his knowledge of the law and his skill in being able to shelter a large portion of your assets that otherwise would have been spent on the nursing home. A written fee agreement is always a good idea, so that each party understands up front what is going to be done, and what the fee will be.

At the initial conference, you need to advise the attorney of the following facts:

Your financial assets, organized by category, and the value of each

Copies of any estate planning documents you have, such as wills, trusts, powers of attorney, etc.

Life insurance policies, including cash value

Income and expense list

Copies of deeds and value of real estate

Value of vehicles

Liabilities

Any special issues affecting your family, such as discord among your children, or whether any of your beneficiaries have special needs

Whether you have made any gifts within the past three years, and, if so, the size of the gifts

Assuming that you supply the attorney with the above information, he should be able to evaluate the situation, and make substantive recommendations, within a fairly short time.

One final, important, element in choosing an attorney is the personal comfort level that each of you has with the other. Although the attorney will be doing the work, a successful attorney-client relationship is actually a partnership between the attorney and client. That is, both of you will be working together under difficult circumstances towards achieving a common goal. Especially if a Medicaid application is involved, you and the attorney will be working closely for a number of months, on some very detailed and perhaps difficult issues. Just as in any relationship, each party needs to keep communications open, and to feel confident with the other.

Chapter 11:

Ten Steps to Take Right Now

When Alzheimer's Disease, or another progressive condition, affects you or a family member, learning as much as possible about the disorder and legal issues that may arise is important. Now that you've reviewed the issues discussed in this book, here is a list of action steps to take right now:

1. Learn all you can about the relevant disease or condition. Ask questions of your doctor. Read books and explore Internet sources.

2. Contact the nearest chapter of the Alzheimer's Association, or other organization relevant to the disease, for additional information, including recent developments in medical research into the cause and treatment of the disease.

3. Join a support group.

4. Discuss your condition and your feelings with family members or a close friend.

5. Schedule an appointment with an experienced Elder Law attorney and immediately begin any planning that needs to be done.

6. Gather the information and documents you'll need to take to the appointment with the Elder Law attorney.

7. Execute durable powers of attorney for financial and health care decisions and an advance directive, as well as any other documents the attorney believes need to be in place.

8. Review your will or trust with the attorney and make any necessary changes. Ask if any Medicaid planning steps should be taken at this time.

9. Make your decisions and wishes concerning financial and personal matters known to your loved ones and doctors.

10. Talk to your doctor about your health care wishes and end-of-life matters. Ask if he or she is comfortable with what you've decided. If not, ask for a referral to another physician who will honor your wishes.

Chapter 12:

End-of-Life Planning

Sleep after toil, port after stormy seas,
   Ease after war, death after life does greatly please.

Edmund Spenser,
The Faerie Queene, (1590)

I n this quotation from the epic, *The Faerie Queene*, the poet Spenser is saying that death is not to be feared. Rather, it provides the rest we all need and deserve after we have accomplished our mission in life. The theme throughout this book has been the benefits of planning, *i.e.*, that if you plan properly, you can control what happens to you, rather than be a passive recipient of what life puts in your way. We continue this theme with our second to final chapter.

It is a fact of life that most people in a nursing home are in the final home they will know. For this reason, it is very important that nursing home patients, while they are still capable, make end-of-life decisions. This is the final gift that they can give to their loved ones. In this type of planning, you designate which loved one will make the ultimate decision about termination of life support, and, generally, you make your wishes known about your transition to death, which Shakespeare called, "The undiscovered country, from whose bourn no traveler returns..." *Hamlet*, Act III.

All states have enacted so-called advance directive statutes, which enable people to make these decisions while they are competent and can discuss them with their loved ones. Preprinted forms for this purpose are available at no charge, or for a nominal charge from hospitals and many senior's centers. These forms are frequently referred to as living wills, health care proxies, or health care powers of attorney. Advance directives essentially state that a person of your choice will have charge of your medical decisions, if you are no longer able to do so. These forms also state that in the event that you are terminally ill and have no chance of recovery, you want all artificial measures removed. Although these documents are largely preprinted forms, and are written in legalistic language, they all have places where your personal wishes can be written. In this way, you can customize these forms to meet your needs, desires and circumstances.

After you have signed the advance directive forms, it is very important that you give copies to your doctors, who will make them a part of your file, and to your spouse and children as well. After all, these forms are of no use if no one knows that you have them. We encourage everyone to sign such documents. Doing so will ease the burdens on your family tremendously, and will be the final, and most important gift that you can give them.

Chapter 13:

Frequently Asked Questions

1. If I go into a nursing home, does the nursing home take all my assets at once, or are my assets frozen?

It is a misconception that your assets are frozen or are seized by the nursing home. Neither happens. Rather, just like any other creditor, the nursing home sends you a bill which you pay each month. The probable source of the misconception that all of your assets are frozen comes from the fact that single people have to spend virtually all of their money, and married people have to spend most of their money, before Medicaid becomes effective. Based on these facts, it is not illogical to think that the nursing home takes all of your money at once, but it doesn't work that way.

2. If I am in the nursing home on Medicaid, do my Social Security and pensions go to the nursing home, or do I still get them?

You still continue to receive all of your income, whether from Social Security, pensions, or any other source. How you have to spend that income, however, depends on such factors as your marital status and your income and expenses. In the case of an unmarried person, all income less a small personal needs allowance ($50 to $60, depending on state) and money to cover health insurance premiums, is required to be paid monthly to the nursing home. Medicaid pays the rest. The same holds true in the case of a married couple; however, depending on the income and needs of the healthy spouse, such spouse may be entitled to an allowance from the nursing home spouse. In this case, the nursing home spouse's income, less the personal needs allowance, health insurance premiums, and spousal allowance, is paid to the nursing home each month.

3. Isn't it true that, in order to protect assets from the nursing home, you need to act either three years or five years in advance?

This is definitely untrue. Although advance planning is better, it is possible to protect a significant amount of assets in far less than three or five years. In the case of a single person, a technique known as a gift trust can shelter roughly 45 to 60% of the assets in a lump sum, even if the person is already in a nursing home or is about to go into one. In the case of a married couple, the Medicaid rules on spenddown and entitlement to income can be used together to protect 100% of the monetary assets, even at the eleventh hour.

4. I have a revocable living trust that I did over three years ago. Aren't my assets protected from the nursing home?

Your assets are probably not protected. Generally speaking, a revocable living trust is designed to avoid probate, and sometimes, estate taxes on your death. Such a trust does not protect assets from the nursing home, regardless of how long ago you did the trust. Some revocable living trusts have provisions known as Medicaid Triggers. These provisions are activated when you go into a nursing home. If they are properly implemented, they can shelter much of your estate from the nursing home.

5. Does a premarital agreement entered into between spouses in a second marriage provide nursing home protection?

Definitely not! Most people think that the assets they bring to a second marriage are protected in case their spouse goes into the nursing home. Similarly, most people think that a premarital agreement, which spells out each party's rights in a second marriage, protects the money. Neither statement is true. The assets of both parties are added together, regardless of whether it is a second marriage or there is a premarital agreement. Generally speaking, the healthy spouse can keep the home and half of the other assets, up to a maximum of about $89,000, regardless of who brought the assets to the marriage. When you say, "I do," you are consenting to your assets becoming part of the spenddown picture.

6. I bought an annuity a number of years ago. Isn't this money protected from the nursing home?

A resounding, "No." Most annuities are not protected from the nursing home, regardless of what the annuity salesperson might have said. An annuity purchased for investment is known as a deferred annuity. You always have the right to cash in a deferred annuity, subject to any surrender penalties. Any asset that can be cashed in is fully subject to the nursing home. The only type of annuity that may be protected from the nursing home is an immediate annuity. This is the type of annuity in which you deposit the money with the annuity company, and the company immediately starts to repay the money to you. This type of annuity is protected only in the case of a married couple in which the healthy party purchases the annuity, and then again, only if the annuity is structured precisely in compliance with exacting state and federal standards.

7. I entered the nursing home some time ago, and used up my money. I am applying for Medicaid. Can the nursing home force me to leave, or otherwise discriminate against me?

No, the nursing home cannot do either. The law states that there can be no difference in treatment between a private pay patient and a Medicaid patient. The only difference between the two is that Medicaid will not pay for a private room. Other than that, the care and treatment received is exactly the same.

8. I want to protect my house in case I go into a nursing home. I have heard that if I put my house into my children's names, it will be protected. Is this true?

Strictly speaking, it is true. However, putting your house in your children's names is the worst method of Medicaid planning, and should rarely, if ever, be done. There are three reasons for this. The first is liability. If your house is in your son's name, for example, and if he gets sued or divorced, then his creditors can put a claim against your house. Second, you lose control over the property, in that you can't sell without your children's permission. If you do sell, the money belongs to your children. Third, your children can lose an important tax advantage. That is, if your children inherit your property at death, and sell it, there will be little, if any capital gains tax. If you put the house in their names during life, however, they lose this tax advantage.

9. I am applying for Medicaid. I have a safe deposit box with cash in it, that no one knows about. Do I have to disclose it on the Medicaid application?

Absolutely. If you intentionally fail to disclose an asset that you know about, you are committing a crime. You should never do this. Many times, however, you file a Medicaid application for one of your relatives. After the relative is on Medicaid, you discover an asset that you just didn't know about when you filed the application. As long as you promptly let Medicaid know about the newly-discovered asset, you are not in any trouble at all. You are only in trouble if you knowingly fail to disclose an asset.

10. I have a Medicaid trust that is subject to a five-year lookback period. I go into the nursing home before the five years have expired. Is the trust effective?

Depending on the amount of assets in the trust, it will either be fully effective or partially effective. That is, the protection afforded by such trusts is not all or nothing. Rather, you take the value of the trust, and divide it by the state's transfer of asset rate in effect. Such rates are generally in the $5,000 to $6,000 per month range. In a $5,500 state, for example, for each month that has gone by since the trust was set up, another $5,500 worth of trust assets will have been protected. After a year, for example, $66,000 (i.e., $5,500 x 12) of the trust assets will have been protected.

Appendix A

Selected Sections from Code of Federal Regulations, Title 42, Part 483, Rights of Nursing Home Patients

I. Sec. 483.10 Resident rights
The resident has a right to a dignified existence, self-determination, and communication with and access to persons and services inside and outside the facility. A facility must protect and promote the rights of each resident, including each of the following rights:

(a) Exercise of rights.

(1) The resident has the right to exercise his or her rights as a resident of the facility and as a citizen or resident of the United States.

(2) The resident has the right to be free of interference, coercion, discrimination, and reprisal from the facility in exercising his or her rights.

(3) In the case of a resident adjudged incompetent under the laws of a State by a court of competent jurisdiction, the rights of the resident are exercised by the person appointed under State law to act on the resident's behalf.

(4) In the case of a resident who has not been adjudged incompetent by the State court, any legal-surrogate designated in accordance with

State law may exercise the resident's rights to the extent provided by State law.

(b) Notice of rights and services.

(1) The facility must inform the resident both orally and in writing in a language that the resident understands of his or her rights and all rules and regulations governing resident conduct and responsibilities during the stay in the facility. The facility must also provide the resident with the notice (if any) of the State developed under section 1919(e)(6) of the Act. Such notification must be made prior to or upon admission and during the resident's stay. Receipt of such information, and any amendments to it, must be acknowledged in writing;

(2) The resident or his or her legal representative has the right-

(i) Upon an oral or written request, to access all records pertaining to himself or herself including current clinical records within 24 hours (excluding weekends and holidays); and

(ii) After receipt of his or her records for inspection, to purchase at a cost not to exceed the community standard photocopies of the records or any portions of them upon request and 2 working days advance notice to the facility.

(3) The resident has the right to be fully informed in language that he or she can understand of his or her total health status, including but not limited to, his or her medical condition;

(4) The resident has the right to refuse treatment, to

refuse to participate in experimental research, and to formulate an advance directive as specified in paragraph (8) of this section; and

(5) The facility must-

(i) Inform each resident who is entitled to Medicaid benefits, in writing, at the time of admission to the nursing facility or, when the resident becomes eligible for Medicaid of-

(A) The items and services that are included in nursing facility services under the State plan and for which the resident may not be charged;

(B) Those other items and services that the facility offers and for which the resident may be charged, and the amount of charges for those services; and

(ii) Inform each resident when changes are made to the items and services specified in paragraphs (5)(i) (A) and (B) of this section.

(6) The facility must inform each resident before, or at the time of admission, and periodically during the resident's stay, of services available in the facility and of charges for those services, including any charges for services not covered under Medicare or by the facility's per diem rate.

(7) The facility must furnish a written description of legal rights which includes-

(i) A description of the manner of protecting personal funds, under paragraph (c) of this section;

(ii) A description of the requirements and procedures for establishing eligibility for Medicaid, including the right to request an assessment under section 1924(c) which determines the extent of a couple's non-exempt resources at the time of institutionalization and attributes to the community spouse an equitable share of resources which cannot be considered available for payment toward the cost of the institutionalized spouse's medical care in his or her process of spending down to Medicaid eligibility levels;

(iii) A posting of names, addresses, and telephone numbers of all pertinent State client advocacy groups such as the State survey and certification agency, the State licensure office, the State ombudsman program, the protection and advocacy network, and the Medicaid fraud control unit; and

(iv) A statement that the resident may file a complaint with the State survey and certification agency concerning resident abuse, neglect, misappropriation of resident property in the facility, and non-compliance with the advance directives requirements.

(8) The facility must comply with the requirements specified in subpart I of part 489 of this chapter relating to maintaining written policies and procedures regarding advance directives. These requirements include provisions to inform and provide written information to all adult residents concerning the right to accept or refuse medical

or surgical treatment and, at the individual's option, formulate an advance directive. This includes a written description of the facility's policies to implement advance directives and applicable State law. Facilities are permitted to contract with other entities to furnish this information but are still legally responsible for ensuring that the requirements of this section are met. If an adult individual is incapacitated at the time of admission and is unable to receive information (due to the incapacitating condition or a mental disorder) or articulate whether or not he or she has executed an advance directive, the facility may give advance directive information to the individual's family or surrogate in the same manner that it issues other materials about policies and procedures to the family of the incapacitated individual or to a surrogate or other concerned persons in accordance with State law. The facility is not relieved of its obligation to provide this information to the individual once he or she is no longer incapacitated or unable to receive such information. Follow-up procedures must be in place to provide the information to the individual directly at the appropriate time.

(9) The facility must inform each resident of the name, specialty, and way of contacting the physician responsible for his or her care.

(10) The facility must prominently display in the facility written information, and provide to residents and applicants for admission oral and

written information about how to apply for and use Medicare and Medicaid benefits, and how to receive refunds for previous payments covered by such benefits.

(11) Notification of changes.

(i) A facility must immediately inform the resident; consult with the resident's physician; and if known, notify the resident's legal representative or an interested family member when there is-

(A) An accident involving the resident which results in injury and has the potential for requiring physician intervention;

(B) A significant change in the resident's physical, mental, or psychosocial status (i.e., a deterioration in health, mental, or psychosocial status in either life-threatening conditions or clinical complications);

(C) A need to alter treatment significantly (i.e., a need to discontinue an existing form of treatment due to adverse consequences, or to commence a new form of treatment); or

(D) A decision to transfer or discharge the resident from the facility as specified in Sec. 483.12(a).

(ii) The facility must also promptly notify the resident and, if known, the resident's legal representative or interested family member when there is-

(A) A change in room or roommate assignment as specified in Sec. 483.15(e)(2); or

(B) A change in resident rights under Federal or

     State law or regulations as specified in paragraph (b)(1) of this section.

(iii) The facility must record and periodically update the address and phone number of the resident's legal representative or interested family member.

(c) Protection of resident funds.

(1) The resident has the right to manage his or her financial affairs, and the facility may not require residents to deposit their personal funds with the facility.

(2) Management of personal funds. Upon written authorization of a resident, the facility must hold, safeguard, manage, and account for the personal funds of the resident deposited with the facility, as specified in paragraphs (c)(3)-(8) of this section.

(3) Deposit of funds.

    (i) Funds in excess of $50. The facility must deposit any resident's personal funds in excess of $50 in an interest bearing account (or accounts) that is separate from any of the facility's operating accounts, and that credits all interest earned on resident's funds to that account. (In pooled accounts, there must be a separate accounting for each resident's share.)

    (ii) Funds less than $50. The facility must maintain a resident's personal funds that do not exceed $50 in a non-interest bearing account, interest-bearing account, or petty cash fund.

(4) Accounting and records. The facility must establish and maintain a system that assures a full

and complete and separate accounting, according to generally accepted accounting principles, of each resident's personal funds entrusted to the facility on the resident's behalf.

(i) The system must preclude any commingling of resident funds with facility funds or with the funds of any person other than another resident.

(ii) The individual financial record must be available through quarterly statements and on request to the resident or his or her legal representative.

(5) Notice of certain balances. The facility must notify each resident that receives Medicaid benefits-

(i) When the amount in the resident's account reaches $200 less than the SSI resource limit for one person, specified in section 1611(a)(3)(B) of the Act; and

(ii) That, if the amount in the account, in addition to the value of the resident's other nonexempt resources, reaches the SSI resource limit for one person, the resident may lose eligibility for Medicaid or SSI.

(6) Conveyance upon death. Upon the death of a resident with a personal fund deposited with the facility, the facility must convey within 30 days the resident's funds, and a final accounting of those funds, to the individual or probate jurisdiction administering the resident's estate.

(7) Assurance of financial security. The facility must purchase a surety bond, or otherwise provide

assurance satisfactory to the Secretary, to assure the security of all personal funds of residents deposited with the facility.

(8) Limitation on charges to personal funds. The facility may not impose a charge against the personal funds of a resident for any item or service for which payment is made under Medicaid or Medicare (except for applicable deductible and coinsurance amounts). The facility may charge the resident for requested services that are more expensive than or in excess of covered services in accordance with Sec. 489.32 of this chapter. (This does not affect the prohibition on facility charges for items and services for which Medicaid has paid. See Sec. 447.15, which limits participation in the Medicaid program to providers who accept, as payment in full, Medicaid payment plus any deductible, coinsurance, or copayment required by the plan to be paid by the individual.)

(i) Services included in Medicare or Medicaid payment. During the course of a covered Medicare or Medicaid stay, facilities may not charge a resident for the following categories of items and services:

(A) Nursing services as required at Sec. 483.30 of this subpart.

(B) Dietary services as required at Sec. 483.35 of this subpart.

(C) An activities program as required at Sec. 483.15(f) of this subpart.

(D) Room/bed maintenance services.

(E) Routine personal hygiene items and services as required to meet the needs of residents, including, but not limited to, hair hygiene supplies, comb, brush, bath soap, disinfecting soaps or specialized cleansing agents when indicated to treat special skin problems or to fight infection, razor, shaving cream, toothbrush, toothpaste, denture adhesive, denture cleaner, dental floss, moisturizing lotion, tissues, cotton balls, cotton swabs, deodorant, incontinence care and supplies, sanitary napkins and related supplies, towels, washcloths, hospital gowns, over the counter drugs, hair and nail hygiene services, bathing, and basic personal laundry.

(F) Medically-related social services as required at Sec. 483.15(g) of this subpart.

(ii) Items and services that may be charged to residents' funds. Listed below are general categories and examples of items and services that the facility may charge to residents' funds if they are requested by a resident, if the facility informs the resident that there will be a charge, and if payment is not made by Medicare or Medicaid:

(A) Telephone.

(B) Television/radio for personal use.

(C) Personal comfort items, including smoking materials, notions and novelties, and confections.

(D) Cosmetic and grooming items and services in

excess of those for which payment is made
under Medicaid or Medicare.

(E) Personal clothing.

(F) Personal reading matter.

(G) Gifts purchased on behalf of a resident.

(H) Flowers and plants.

(I) Social events and entertainment offered outside the scope of the activities program, provided under Sec. 483.15(f) of this subpart.

(J) Noncovered special care services such as privately hired nurses or aides.

(K) Private room, except when therapeutically
required (for example, isolation for infection
control).

(L) Specially prepared or alternative food
requested instead of the food generally prepared by the facility, as required by Sec.
483.35 of this subpart.

(iii) Requests for items and services.

(A) The facility must not charge a resident (or
his or her representative) for any item or
service not requested by the resident.

(B) The facility must not require a resident (or
his or her representative) to request any item
or service as a condition of admission or
continued stay.

(C) The facility must inform the resident (or his or
her representative) requesting an item or service for which a charge will be made that there
will be a charge for the item or service and
what the charge will be.

(D) Free choice. The resident has the right to—
(1) Choose a personal attending physician;
(2) Be fully informed in advance about care and treatment and of any changes in that care or treatment that may affect the resident's well-being; and
(3) Unless adjudged incompetent or otherwise found to be incapacitated under the laws of the State, participate in planning care and treatment or changes in care and treatment.

(E) Privacy and confidentiality. The resident has the right to personal privacy and confidentiality of his or her personal and clinical records.
(1) Personal privacy includes accommodations, medical treatment, written and telephone communications, personal care, visits, and meetings of family and resident groups, but this does not require the facility to provide a private room for each resident;
(2) Except as provided in paragraph (e)(3) of this section, the resident may approve or refuse the release of personal and clinical records to any individual outside the facility;
(3) The resident's right to refuse release of personal and clinical records does not apply when:
(i) The resident is transferred to another health care institution; or

(ii) Record release is required by law.
(F) Grievances. A resident has the right to:
   (1) Voice grievances without discrimination or reprisal. Such grievances include those with respect to treatment which has been furnished as well as that which has not been furnished; and
   (2) Prompt efforts by the facility to resolve grievances the resident may have, including those with respect to the behavior of other residents.
(G) Examination of survey results. A resident has the right to-
   (1) Examine the results of the most recent survey of the facility conducted by Federal or State surveyors and any plan of correction in effect with respect to the facility. The facility must make the results available for examination in a place readily accessible to residents, and must post a notice of their availability; and
   (2) Receive information from agencies acting as client advocates, and be afforded the opportunity to contact these agencies.
(H) Work. The resident has the right to:
   (1) Refuse to perform services for the facility;
   (2) Perform services for the facility, if he or she chooses, when:
      (i) The facility has documented the need or desire for work in the plan of care;
      (ii) The plan specifies the nature of the serv-

ices performed and whether the services
are voluntary or paid;

(iii) Compensation for paid services is at or
above prevailing rates; and

(iv) The resident agrees to the work
arrangement described in the plan of
care.

(I) Mail. The resident has the right to privacy in
written communications, including the right
to:

(1) Send and promptly receive mail that is
unopened; and

(2) Have access to stationery, postage, and
writing implements at the resident's own
expense.

(J) Access and visitation rights.

(1) The resident has the right and the facility
must provide immediate access to any resident by the following:

(i) Any representative of the Secretary;

(ii) Any representative of the State:

(iii) The resident's individual physician;

(iv) The State long term care ombudsman
(established under section 307(a)(12)
of the Older Americans Act of 1965);

(v) The agency responsible for the protection
and advocacy system for developmental-
ly disabled individuals (established
under part C of the Developmental
Disabilities Assistance and Bill of Rights
Act);

(vi) The agency responsible for the protection and advocacy system for mentally ill individuals (established under the Protection and Advocacy for Mentally Ill Individuals Act);

(vii) Subject to the resident's right to deny or withdraw consent at any time, immediate family or other relatives of the resident; and

(viii) Subject to reasonable restrictions and the resident's right to deny or withdraw consent at any time, others who are visiting with the consent of the resident.

(2) The facility must provide reasonable access to any resident by any entity or individual that provides health, social, legal, or other services to the resident, subject to the resident's right to deny or withdraw consent at any time.

(3) The facility must allow representatives of the State Ombudsman, described in paragraph (j)(1)(iv) of this section, to examine a resident's clinical records with the permission of the resident or the resident's legal representative, and consistent with State law.

(K) Telephone. The resident has the right to have reasonable access to the use of a telephone where calls can be made without being overheard.

(L) Personal property. The resident has the right to retain and use personal possessions, including some furnishings, and appropriate clothing, as space permits, unless to do so would infringe upon the rights or health and safety of other residents.

(M) Married couples. The resident has the right to share a room with his or her spouse when married residents live in the same facility and both spouses consent to the arrangement.

(N) Self-Administration of Drugs. An individual resident may self-administer drugs if the interdisciplinary team, as defined by Sec. 483.20(d)(2)(ii), has determined that this practice is safe.

(O) Refusal of certain transfers.

(1) An individual has the right to refuse a transfer to another room within the institution, if the purpose of the transfer is to relocate—

(i) A resident of a SNF from the distinct part of the institution that is a SNF to a part of the institution that is not a SNF, or

(ii) A resident of a NF from the distinct part of the institution that is a NF to a distinct part of the institution that is a SNF.

(2) A resident's exercise of the right to refuse transfer under paragraph (o)(1) of this section does not affect the individual's eligibility or entitlement to Medicare or Medicaid benefits.

II. Sec. 483.15 Quality of life

A facility must care for its residents in a manner and in an environment that promotes maintenance or enhancement of each resident's quality of life.

(a) Dignity. The facility must promote care for residents in a manner and in an environment that maintains or enhances each resident's dignity and respect in full recognition of his or her individuality.

(b) Self-determination and participation. The resident has the right to-

   (1) Choose activities, schedules, and health care consistent with his or her interests, assessments, and plans of care;

   (2) Interact with members of the community both inside and outside the facility; and

   (3) Make choices about aspects of his or her life in the facility that are significant to the resident.

(c) Participation in resident and family groups.

   (1) A resident has the right to organize and participate in resident groups in the facility;

   (2) A resident's family has the right to meet in the facility with the families of other residents in the facility;

   (3) The facility must provide a resident or family group, if one exists, with private space;

   (4) Staff or visitors may attend meetings at the group's invitation;

   (5) The facility must provide a designated staff person responsible for providing assistance and responding to written requests that result from group meetings;

(6) When a resident or family group exists, the facility must listen to the views and act upon the grievances and recommendations of residents and families concerning proposed policy and operational decisions affecting resident care and life in the facility.

(d) Participation in other activities. A resident has the right to participate in social, religious, and community activities that do not interfere with the rights of other residents in the facility.

(e) Accommodation of needs. A resident has the right to:

(1) Reside and receive services in the facility with reasonable accommodation of individual needs and preferences, except when the health or safety of the individual or other residents would be endangered; and

(2) Receive notice before the resident's room or roommate in the facility is changed.

(f) Activities.

(1) The facility must provide for an ongoing program of activities designed to meet, in accordance with the comprehensive assessment, the interests and the physical, mental, and psychosocial well-being of each resident.

(2) The activities program must be directed by a qualified professional who-

(i) Is a qualified therapeutic recreation specialist or an activities professional who—

(A) Is licensed or registered, if applicable, by the State in which practicing; and

(B) Is eligible for certification as a therapeutic recreation specialist or as an activities professional by a recognized accrediting body on or after October 1, 1990; or

(ii) Has 2 years of experience in a social or recreational program within the last 5 years, 1 of which was full-time in a patient activities program in a health care setting; or

(iii) Is a qualified occupational therapist or occupational therapy assistant; or

(iv) Has completed a training course approved by the State.

(g) Social Services.

(1) The facility must provide medically-related social services to attain or maintain the highest practicable physical, mental, and psychosocial well-being of each resident.

(2) A facility with more than 120 beds must employ a qualified social worker on a full-time basis.

(3) Qualifications of social worker. A qualified social worker is an individual with-

(i) A bachelor's degree in social work or a bachelor's degree in a human services field including but not limited to sociology, special education, rehabilitation counseling, and psychology; and

(ii) One year of supervised social work experience in a health care setting working directly with individuals.

(h) Environment. The facility must provide-

(1) A safe, clean, comfortable, and homelike environment, allowing the resident to use his or her

personal belongings to the extent possible;

(2) Housekeeping and maintenance services necessary to maintain a sanitary, orderly, and comfortable interior;

(3) Clean bed and bath linens that are in good condition;

(4) Private closet space in each resident room, as specified in Sec. 483.70(d)(2)(iv) of this part;

(5) Adequate and comfortable lighting levels in all areas;

(6) Comfortable and safe temperature levels. Facilities initially certified after October 1, 1990 must maintain a temperature range of 71- 81 deg.F; and

(7) For the maintenance of comfortable sound levels.

III. Sec. 483.30 Nursing services
The facility must have sufficient nursing staff to provide nursing and related services to attain or maintain the highest practicable physical, mental, and psychosocial well-being of each resident, as determined by resident assessments and individual plans of care.

(a) Sufficient staff.

(1) The facility must provide services by sufficient numbers of each of the following types of personnel on a 24-hour basis to provide nursing care to all residents in accordance with resident care plans:

(i) Except when waived under paragraph (c) of this section, licensed nurses; and

(ii) Other nursing personnel.

(2) Except when waived under paragraph (c) of this section, the facility must designate a licensed nurse to serve as a charge nurse on each tour of duty.

(b) Registered nurse.

(1) Except when waived under paragraph (c) or (d) of this section, the facility must use the services of a registered nurse for at least 8 consecutive hours a day, 7 days a week.

(2) Except when waived under paragraph (c) or (d) of this section, the facility must designate a registered nurse to serve as the director of nursing on a full time basis.

(3) The director of nursing may serve as a charge nurse only when the facility has an average daily occupancy of 60 or fewer residents.

(c) Nursing facilities: Waiver of requirement to provide licensed nurses on a 24-hour basis. To the extent that a facility is unable to meet the requirements of paragraphs (a)(2) and (b)(1) of this section, a State may waive such requirements with respect to the facility if—

(1) The facility demonstrates to the satisfaction of the State that the facility has been unable, despite diligent efforts (including offering wages at the community prevailing rate for nursing facilities), to recruit appropriate personnel;

(2) The State determines that a waiver of the requirement will not endanger the health or safety of individuals staying in the facility;

(3) The State finds that, for any periods in which

licensed nursing services are not available, a registered nurse or a physician is obligated to respond immediately to telephone calls from the facility;

(4) A waiver granted under the conditions listed in paragraph (c) of this section is subject to annual State review;

(5) In granting or renewing a waiver, a facility may be required by the State to use other qualified, licensed personnel;

(6) The State agency granting a waiver of such requirements provides notice of the waiver to the State long term care ombudsman (established under section 307(a)(12) of the Older Americans Act of 1965) and the protection and advocacy system in the State for the mentally ill and mentally retarded; and

(7) The nursing facility that is granted such a waiver by a State notifies residents of the facility (or, where appropriate, the guardians or legal representatives of such residents) and members of their immediate families of the waiver.

(d) SNFs: Waiver of the requirement to provide services of a registered nurse for more than 40 hours a week.

(1) The Secretary may waive the requirement that a SNF provide the services of a registered nurse for more than 40 hours a week, including a director of nursing specified in paragraph (b) of this section, if the Secretary finds that-

(i) The facility is located in a rural area and the

supply of skilled nursing facility services in the area is not sufficient to meet the needs of individuals residing in the area;

(ii) The facility has one full-time registered nurse who is regularly on duty at the facility 40 hours a week; and

(iii) The facility either-

(A) Has only patients whose physicians have indicated (through physicians' orders or admission notes) that they do not require the services of a registered nurse or a physician for a 48-hour period, or

(B) Has made arrangements for a registered nurse or a physician to spend time at the facility, as determined necessary by the physician, to provide necessary skilled nursing services on days when the regular full-time registered nurse is not on duty;

(iv) The Secretary provides notice of the waiver to the State long term care ombudsman (established under section 307(a)(12) of the Older Americans Act of 1965) and the protection and advocacy system in the State for the mentally ill and mentally retarded; and

(v) The facility that is granted such a waiver notifies residents of the facility (or, where appropriate, the guardians or legal representatives of such residents) and members of their immediate families of the waiver.

(2) A waiver of the registered nurse requirement under paragraph (d)(1) of this section is subject

to annual renewal by the Secretary.

IV. Sec. 483.12 Admission, transfer and discharge rights
  (a) Transfer and discharge-
    (1) Definition: Transfer and discharge includes move-
        ment of a resident to a bed outside of the certi-
        fied facility whether that bed is in the same
        physical plant or not. Transfer and discharge
        does not refer to movement of a resident to a bed
        within the same certified facility.
    (2) Transfer and discharge requirements. The facility
        must permit each resident to remain in the facili-
        ty, and not transfer or discharge the resident
        from the facility unless-
      (i) The transfer or discharge is necessary for the
          resident's welfare and the resident's needs can-
          not be met in the facility;
      (ii) The transfer or discharge is appropriate
          because the resident's health has improved
          sufficiently so the resident no longer needs the
          services provided by the facility;
      (iii) The safety of individuals in the facility is
          endangered;
      (iv) The health of individuals in the facility would
          otherwise be endangered;
      (v) The resident has failed, after reasonable and
          appropriate notice, to pay for (or to have paid
          under Medicare or Medicaid) a stay at the facil-
          ity. For a resident who becomes eligible for
          Medicaid after admission to a facility, the facili-
          ty may charge a resident only allowable

charges under Medicaid; or

(vi) The facility ceases to operate.

(3) Documentation. When the facility transfers or discharges a resident under any of the circumstances specified in paragraphs (a)(2)(i) through (v) of this section, the resident's clinical record must be documented. The documentation must be made by-

(i) The resident's physician when transfer or discharge is necessary under paragraph (a)(2)(i) or paragraph (a)(2)(ii) of this section; and

(ii) A physician when transfer or discharge is necessary under paragraph (a)(2)(iv) of this section.

(4) Notice before transfer. Before a facility transfers or discharges a resident, the facility must-

(i) Notify the resident and, if known, a family member or legal representative of the resident of the transfer or discharge and the reasons for the move in writing and in a language and manner they understand.

(ii) Record the reasons in the resident's clinical record; and

(iii) Include in the notice the items described in paragraph (a)(6) of this section.

(5) Timing of the notice.

(i) Except when specified in paragraph (a)(5)(ii) of this section, the notice of transfer or discharge required under paragraph (a)(4) of this section must be made by the facility at least 30 days before the resident is transferred or discharged.

(ii) Notice may be made as soon as practicable before transfer or discharge when-

(A) the safety of individuals in the facility would be endangered under paragraph (a)(2)(iii) of this section;

(B) The health of individuals in the facility would be endangered, under paragraph (a)(2)(iv) of this section;

(C) The resident's health improves sufficiently to allow a more immediate transfer or discharge, under paragraph (a)(2)(ii) of this section;

(D) An immediate transfer or discharge is required by the resident's urgent medical needs, under paragraph (a)(2)(i) of this section; or

(E) A resident has not resided in the facility for 30 days.

(6) Contents of the notice. The written notice specified in paragraph (a)(4) of this section must include the following:

(i) The reason for transfer or discharge;

(ii) The effective date of transfer or discharge;

(iii) The location to which the resident is transferred or discharged;

(iv) A statement that the resident has the right to appeal the action to the State;

(v) The name, address and telephone number of the State long term care ombudsman;

(vi) For nursing facility residents with developmental disabilities, the mailing address and

telephone number of the agency responsible
for the protection and advocacy of develop-
mentally disabled individuals established
under Part C of the Developmental Disabilities
Assistance and Bill of Rights Act; and

(vii) For nursing facility residents who are mentally ill, the mailing address and telephone number of the agency responsible for the protection and advocacy of mentally ill individuals
established under the Protection and
Advocacy for Mentally Ill Individuals Act.

(7) Orientation for transfer or discharge. A facility
must provide sufficient preparation and orientation to residents to ensure safe and orderly transfer or discharge from the facility.

(b) Notice of bed-hold policy and readmission—

(1) Notice before transfer. Before a nursing facility
transfers a resident to a hospital or allows a resident to go on therapeutic leave, the nursing facility must provide written information to the resident and a family member or legal representative
that specifies—

(i) The duration of the bed-hold policy under the
State plan, if any, during which the resident is
permitted to return and resume residence in the
nursing facility; and

(ii) The nursing facility's policies regarding bed-
hold periods, which must be consistent with
paragraph (b)(3) of this section, permitting a
resident to return.

(2) Bed-hold notice upon transfer. At the time of

transfer of a resident for hospitalization or therapeutic leave, a nursing facility must provide to
the resident and a family member or legal representative written notice which specifies the duration of the bed-hold policy described in paragraph (b)(1) of this section.

(3) Permitting resident to return to facility. A nursing
facility must establish and follow a written policy
under which a resident, whose hospitalization or
therapeutic leave exceeds the bed-hold period
under the State plan, is readmitted to the facility
immediately upon the first availability of a bed in
a semi-private room if the resident-
   (i) Requires the services provided by the facility;
   and
   (ii) Is eligible for Medicaid nursing facility services.
(c) Equal access to quality care.
   (1) A facility must establish and maintain identical
   policies and practices regarding transfer, discharge, and the provision of services under the
   State plan for all individuals regardless of source
   of payment;
   (2) The facility may charge any amount for services
   furnished to non-Medicaid residents consistent
   with the notice requirement in Sec. 483.10(b)(5)(i)
   and (b)(6) describing the charges; and
   (3) The State is not required to offer additional services on behalf of a resident other than services
   provided in the State plan.
(d) Admissions policy.
   (1) The facility must-

(i) Not require residents or potential residents to waive their rights to Medicare or Medicaid; and

(ii) Not require oral or written assurance that residents or potential residents are not eligible for, or will not apply for, Medicare or Medicaid benefits.

(2) The facility must not require a third party guarantee of payment to the facility as a condition of admission or expedited admission, or continued stay in the facility. However, the facility may require an individual who has legal access to a resident's income or resources available to pay for facility care to sign a contract, without incurring personal financial liability, to provide facility payment from the resident's income or resources.

(3) In the case of a person eligible for Medicaid, a nursing facility must not charge, solicit, accept, or receive, in addition to any amount otherwise required to be paid under the State plan, any gift, money, donation, or other consideration as a precondition of admission, expedited admission or continued stay in the facility. However,—

(i) A nursing facility may charge a resident who is eligible for Medicaid for items and services the resident has requested and received, and that are not specified in the State plan as included in the term "nursing facility services" so long as the facility gives proper notice of the availability and cost of these services to residents and does not condition the resident's admission or continued stay on the request for and receipt of such additional services; and

(ii) A nursing facility may solicit, accept, or receive a charitable, religious, or philanthropic contribution from an organization or from a person unrelated to a Medicaid eligible resident or potential resident, but only to the extent that the contribution is not a condition of admission, expedited admission, or continued stay in the facility for a Medicaid eligible resident.

(4) States or political subdivisions may apply stricter admissions standards under State or local laws than are specified in this section, to prohibit discrimination against individuals entitled to Medicaid.

Appendix B
Helpful Addresses and Phone Numbers

C ontact your state office on aging for help finding services for older citizens and for information about a needs assessment required for a Medicaid waiver program. Your state Medicaid agency administers the program for eligible persons, including long-term care in a nursing home. For questions about how to request a review of driving privileges for someone who might have Alzheimer's Disease, contact the driver's licensing division of your state's motor vehicle administration.

Addresses are listed by state in the order of: the office on aging, Medicaid agency and driver's license authority.

Alabama
Office on Aging
Commission of Aging
RSA Plz., Suite 470
770 Washington Ave.
Montgomery, AL 36130

Medicaid Agency
Medicaid Agency
PO Box 5624
Montgomery, AL 36103- 5624

Driver's License Authority
Driver License Division
Dep't. of Public Safety
500 Dexter Ave, PO Box 1471
Montgomery, AL 36102

Alaska

Office on Aging
Commission on Aging
Dep't. of Administration
PO Box 110209
Juneau, AK 99811-0209

Medicaid Agency
Division of Medical Assistance
PO Box 110660
Juneau, AK 99811-0660

Driver's License Authority
Division of Motor Vehicles
Dep't. of Administration
5700 E. Tudor Rd.
Anchorage, AK 99507-1225

Arizona

Office on Aging
Aging and Adult Administration
Dep't. of Economic Security
1789 W. Jefferson
Phoenix, AZ 85007

Medicaid Agency
Health Care Cost Containment
  System
801 E. Jefferson
Phoenix, AZ 85007

Driver's License Authority
Motor Vehicles Div.
Dep't. of Transportation
1801 W. Jefferson
Phoenix, AZ 85007

Arkansas

Office on Aging
Aging and Adult Services
PO Box 1437
Little Rock, AR 72203

Medicaid Agency
Division of Medical Services
Dep't. of Human Services
PO Box 1437, Slot 316
Little Rock, AR 72203

Driver's License Authority
Policy and Legal Revenue
  Division
Dep't. of Finance and
  Administration
PO Box 1272
Little Rock, AR 72203

California

Office on Aging
Dep't. of Aging
1600 K Street
Sacramento, CA 95814

Medicaid Agency
Medi-Cal Operations Division
Dep't. of Health Services
PO Box 942732
Sacramento, CA 95814

Driver's License Authority
Headquarters Operation
Dep't. of Motor Vehicles
PO Box 932328
Sacramento, CA 94232-3280

Colorado

Office on Aging
Aging and Adult Services
  Division
Dep't. of Human Services
110 16th St., 2nd Floor
Denver, CO 80203

Medicaid Agency
Office of Medical Assistance
Health Care Policy and Finance
1575 Sherman, 4th Floor
Denver, CO 80203

Driver's License Authority
Division of Motor Vehicles
  Hearings
Dep't. of Revenue
Denver, CO 80261-0016

Connecticut

Office on Aging
Commission on Aging
25 Sigourney St., 8th Floor
Hartford, CT 06106-5003

Medicaid Agency
Health Care Financing
Dep't. of Social Services
25 Sigourney St., 8th Floor
Hartford, CT 06106-5003

Driver's License Authority
Dep't. of Motor Vehicles
60 State St.
Wethersfield, CT 06109

Delaware

Office on Aging
Division of Aging and Physically
  Handicapped
Health and Social Services Dep't.
1901 N. DuPont Hwy.
New Castle, DE 19720

Medicaid Agency
Division of Social Services
  Medicaid Unit
DHSS Main Campus
1901 N. DuPont Hwy.
New Castle, DE 19720

Driver's License Authority
Division of Motor Vehicles
Dep't. of Public Safety
PO Box 698
Dover, DE 19903

District of Columbia

Office on Aging
Office on Aging
441 4th St., NW
Washington, DC 20001

Medicaid Agency
Health Care Finance
Dep't. of Human Services
2100 M.L. King, Jr. Ave., SE
Washington, DC 20020-5732

Driver's License Authority
Bureau of Motor Vehicle Services
Municipal Center
301 C St. NW
Washington, DC 20001

Florida
Office on Aging
Dep't. of Elder Affairs
Bldg. E, Rm. 317
1317 Winewood Blvd.
Tallahassee, FL 32399-0700

Medicaid Agency
Bureau of Medicaid
Agency for Health Care
  Administration
2727 Mahan Dr.
Tallahassee, FL 32308

Driver's License Authority
Motor Vehicles Division
Highway Safety and Motor
  Vehicles
2900 Neil Kirkman Bldg.
2900 Apalachee Pkwy
Tallahassee, FL 32399-0500

Georgia
Office on Aging
Division of Aging Services
Dep't. of Human Resources
Room 36-385
2 Peachtree St., NW
Atlanta, GA 30303

Medicaid Agency
Dep't. of Medical Assistance
Suite 4043
2 Peachtree St.
Atlanta, GA 30303

Driver's License Authority
Motor Vehicle Division
Room 104
270 Washington St. SW
Atlanta, GA 30303

Hawaii
Office on Aging
Office of the Governor
Executive Office on Aging
Suite 107
250 S. Hotel St.
Honolulu, HI 96813-2831

Medicaid Agency
Dep't. of Human Services
1390 Miller St.
Honolulu, HI 96813

Driver's License Authority
Driver's License Section
PO Box 30340
Honolulu, HI 96820

Idaho
Office on Aging
Office on Aging
Statehouse, Room 108
700 W. Jefferson
Boise, ID 83720

Medicaid Agency
Idaho Health and Welfare
Dep't. of Medicaid
Suite 230
3380 Americana Terrace
PO Box 83720
Boise, ID 83720-0036

Driver's License Authority
Motor Vehicle Bureau
Dep't. of Transportation
PO Box 7129
Boise, ID 83707-1129

Illinois
Office on Aging
Dep't. on Aging
421 E. Capitol
Springfield, IL 62701

Medicaid Agency
Dep't. of Public Aid
201 S. Grand Ave.
E. Springfield, IL 62762

Driver's License Authority
Secretary of State Medical
   Review
2701 S. Dirksen Pkwy.
Springfield, IL 62723

Indiana
Office on Aging
Division of Aging and
   Rehabilitation
Family and Social Services
   Administration
Room W451
402 W. Washington
Indianapolis, IN 46204

Medicaid Agency
Medicaid Policy and Planning
Family and Social Services
   Administration
Room W382, IGC-S
Indianapolis, IN 46204

Driver's License Authority
Bureau of Motor Vehicles
IGC-North, Rm. 440
Indianapolis, IN 46204

Iowa
Office on Aging
Dep't. of Elder Affairs
200 10th St.
Des Moines, IA 50309-3609

Medicaid Agency
Medical Services Division
Dep't. of Human Services
Hoover State Office Building
1300 E. Walnut
Des Moines, IA 50319

Driver's License Authority
Motor Vehicle Division
Dep't. of Transportation
PO Box 10382
Des Moines, IA 50306

Kansas

Office on Aging
Dep't. of Aging
Docking State Office Building
Room 150-S
300 SW l0th St.
Topeka, KS 66612-1500

Medicaid Agency
Adult and Medical Services
Social and Rehab. Services
Docking Office Bldg
Room 628-S
915 Harrison
Topeka, KS 66612-1570

Driver's License Authority
Division of Vehicles
Dep't. of Revenue
Docking State Office
Building, Room 162-S
915 Harrison St.
Topeka, KS 66626-0001

Kentucky
Office on Aging
Division of Aging Services
Dep't. for Social Services
275 E. Main St., 5 W
Frankfort, KY 40621

Medicaid Agency
Health Services Cabinet
275 E. Main St.
Frankfort, KY 40621

Driver's License Authority
Transportation Dep't.
Dep't. of Vehicle Regulation
State Office Building Room 308
501 High St.
Frankfort, KY 40601

Louisiana
Office on Aging
Office of Elderly Affairs
PO Box 80374
Baton Rouge, LA 70898

Medicaid Agency
Bureau of Health Services
   Financing
Dep't. of Health and Hospitals
PO Box 91030
Baton Rouge, LA 70821

Driver's License Authority
Office of Motor Vehicles
Public Safety and Corrections
   Dep't.
PO Box 66614
Baton Rouge, LA 70896

Maine
Office on Aging
Bureau of Elderly and Adult
   Services
Dep't. of Human Services
11 State House Station
Augusta, ME 04333

Medicaid Agency
Bureau of Medical Services
Dep't. of Human Services
11 State House Station
Augusta, ME 04333

Driver's License Authority
Division of Motor Vehicles
Dep't. of State
29 State House Station
Augusta, ME 04333

Maryland

Office on Aging
Office on Aging
301 W. Preston St. Room 1007
Baltimore, MD 21201

Medicaid Agency
Medical Care Finance and
   Compliance Admin.
Dep't. of Health and Mental
   Hygiene
201 W. Preston St. 2nd Floor
Baltimore, MD 21201

Driver's License Authority
Motor Vehicle Administration
MD Dep't. of Transportation
6601 Ritchie Hwy., NE, Room
    120
Glen Burnie, MD 21062

Massachusetts
Office on Aging
Executive Office of Elder Affairs
1 Ashburton PL., 5th Floor,
    Room 517
Boston, MA 02108

Medicaid Agency
Executive Office of Health and
    Human Services
Dep't. of Transitional Assistance
600 Washington St., 6th Floor
Boston, MA 02111

Driver's License Authority
Registry of Motor
    Vehicles/Medical Affairs
PO Box 199100
Boston, MA 02119

Michigan
Office on Aging
Office of Services to the Aging
Dep't. of Community Health
611 W. Ottawa St.
Lansing, MI 48909

Medicaid Agency
Medical Services Administration
Dep't. of Community Health
PO Box 30037
Lansing, MI 48909

Driver's License Authority
Dep't. of State
Driver Assessment Support Unit
7064 Crowner Drive
Lansing, MI 48918

Minnesota
Office on Aging
Board on Aging
Human Services Building, 4th
    Floor
444 Lafayette Rd.
St. Paul, MN 55155

Medicaid Agency
Health Care Dep't. of Human
    Services
444 Lafayette Rd.
St. Paul, MN 55155-3852

Driver's License Authority
Driver and Vehicle Services
    Division
Dep't. of Public Safety
445 Minnesota St., Suite 195
St. Paul, MN 55101-5195

Mississippi
Office on Aging
Council on Aging
Dep't. of Human Services
PO Box 352
Jackson, MS 39205-0352

Medicaid Agency
Division of Medicaid
Office of the Governor
239 N. Lamar St., Suite 801
Jackson, MS 39215-1399

Driver's License Authority
Motor Vehicle Commission
1755 Lelia Dr., Suite 200
PO Box 16873
Jackson, MS 39236

Missouri
Office on Aging
Division of Aging
Dep't. of Social Services
615 Howerton Ct.
PO Box 1337
Jefferson City, MO 65102

Medicaid Agency
Division of Medical Service
Dep't. of Social Services
615 Howerton Ct.
PO Box 6500
Jefferson City, MO 65102- 6500

Driver's License Authority
Division of Motor Vehicles and
    Drivers Licensing
PO Box 200
Jefferson City, MO 65105-0200

Montana
Office on Aging
Aging Services Bureau
Dep't. of Public Health and
    Human Services
111 Sanders St., Room 210
Helena, MT 59620

Medicaid Agency
Health Policy and Services Division
Dep't. of Public Health and
    Human Services
1400 Broadway, Room A206
Helena, MT. 59620

Driver's License Authority
Dep't. of Justice
Motor Vehicle Division
Attention: Medical Dep't.
303 N. Roberts
PO Box 201430
Helena, MT 59620-1430

Nebraska
Office on Aging
Dep't. of Health and Human
    Services
PO Box 95044
Lincoln, NE 68509-5044

Medicaid Agency
Dep't. of Health and Human
    Services
Finance and Support
PO Box 95026
Lincoln, NE 68509

Driver's License Authority
Dep't. of Motor Vehicles
PO Box 94789
Lincoln, NE 68509-4789

Nevada
Office on Aging
Division for Aging Services
340 N. 11 th St., Suite 203
Las Vegas, NV 89101

Medicaid Agency
Medicaid Division
Dep't. of Human Resources
2527 N. Carson St.
Carson City, NV 89701

Driver's License Authority
Dep't. of Motor Vehicles and
Public Safety
555 Wright Way
Carson City, NV 89711-0900

New Hampshire
Office on Aging
Division of Elderly and Adult
Services
Dep't. of Health and Human
Services
Annex Bldg. #1
115 Pleasant St.
Concord, NH 03301-3843

Medicaid Agency
Office of Health Management
6 Hazen Drive
Concord, NH 03301-6527

Driver's License Authority
Division of Motor Vehicles
Dep't. of Safety
10 Hazen Drive
Concord, NH 03301

New Jersey
Office on Aging
Division of Senior Affairs
101 South Broad St
PO Box 807
Trenton, NJ 08625-0807

Medicaid Agency
Dep't. of Human Services
222 S. Warren St.
PO Box 700
Trenton, NJ 08625-0700

Driver's License Authority
Division of Motor Vehicle
Services
Dep't. of Law and Public Safety
225 East State St
PO Box 160
Trenton, NJ 08625-0160

New Mexico
Office on Aging
State Agency on Aging
228 East Palace Avenue
Santa Fe, NM 87503

Medicaid Agency
Medical Assistance Division
Dep't. of Human Services
PO Box 2348
Santa Fe, NM 87503

Driver's License Authority
Motor Vehicle Division
Dep't. of Taxation and Revenue
PO Box 1028
Santa Fe, NM 87504-1028

New York
Office on Aging
5th Floor, Agency Bldg.
Empire State Plaza
Albany, NY 12223-0001

Medicaid Agency
Office of Temporary and
Disability Assistance
16th Floor, 40 N. Pearl St.
Albany, NY 12243

Driver's License Authority
Dep't. of Motor Vehicles
5th Floor
Swan Bldg.
Empire State Plaza
Albany, NY 12228

North Carolina
Office on Aging
Aging Division
Dep't. of Health and Human
    Services
101 Blair Drive
Raleigh, NC 27603

Medicaid Agency
Division of Medical Assistance
Dep't. of Human Resources
1985 Umstead Drive
Raleigh, NC 27603-2001

Driver's License Authority
Division of Motor Vehicles
Dep't. of Transportation
1100 New Bern Ave.
Raleigh, NC 27697-0001

North Dakota
Office on Aging
Aging Services Division
Dep't. of Human Services
Suite 1C, 600 South 2nd St.
Bismark, ND 58504-5729

Medicaid Agency
Medical Services Division
Dep't. of Human Services
600 East Blvd. Avenue
3rd Floor, Judicial Wing
Bismark, ND 58505-0250

Driver's License Authority
Driver License and Traffic Safety
    Division
Dep't. of Transportation
608 East Blvd. Avenue
Bismark, ND 58505-0700

Ohio
Office on Aging
Commission on Aging
Dep't. of Aging
9th Floor, 50 West Broad St.
Columbus, OH 43226

Medicaid Agency
Office of Medicaid
Dep't. of Human Services
31st Floor
30 East Broad St.
Columbus, OH 43215

Driver's License Authority
Bureau of Motor Vehicles
Dep't. of Public Safety
4300 Kimberly Parkway
Columbus, OH 43232-0801

Oklahoma
Office on Aging
Health and Human Services
Dep't. of Human Services
PO Box 25352
Oklahoma City, OK 73125-0352

Medicaid Agency
Health and Human Services
Dep't. of Human Services
PO Box 25352
Oklahoma City, OK 73125-0352

Driver's License Authority
Motor Vehicle Division
Tax Commission
Suite 183
4334 NW Expressway
Oklahoma City, OK 73116

Oregon
Office on Aging
Senior and Disabled Services
    Division
Dep't. of Human Resources
2nd Floor, 500 Summer Street
    NE
Salem, OR 97310-1015

Medicaid Agency
Office of Medical Assistance
    Program
Dep't. of Human Resources
500 Summer St NE
Salem, OR 97310-1014

Driver's License Authority
Motor Vehicles Division
Dep't. of Transportation
1905 Lana Avenue NE
Salem, OR 97314

Pennsylvania
Office on Aging
Dep't. of Aging
Rachel Carson State Office
    Building
6th Floor
400 Market St.
Harrisburg, PA 17102-2675

Medicaid Agency
Medical Assistance
Dep't. of Public Welfare
PO Box 2675
Harrisburg, PA 17105-2675

Driver's License Authority
Bureau of Motor Vehicles
Dep't. of Transportation
4th Floor
1101 S. Front Street
Harrisburg, PA 17104

Rhode Island
Office on Aging
Dep't. of Elderly Affairs
160 Pine Street
Providence, RI 02903

Medicaid Agency
Medical Services
Dep't. of Mental Health &
    Rehabilitation
600 New London Avenue
Cranston, RI 02920

Driver's License Authority
Division of Motor Vehicles
286 Main Street
Pawtucket, RI 02860

South Carolina
Office on Aging
Division of Aging
202 Arbor Lane Drive
Columbia, SC 29223

Medicaid Agency
Dep't. of Health & Human
  Services
PO Box 8206
Columbia, SC 29202

Driver's License Authority
Dep't. of Public Safety
5410 Broad River Road
Columbia, SC 29210

South Dakota
Office on Aging
Division of Adult Services &
  Aging
Dep't. of Social Services
Kneip Bldg.
700 Governors Drive
Pierre, SD 57501

Medicaid Agency
Division of Medical Services
Dep't. of Social Services
700 Governors Drive
Pierre, SD 57501

Driver's License Authority
Division of Driver's Licensing
Dep't. of Commerce & Regulation
Public Safety Bldg.
118 W. Capitol Ave.
Pierre, SD 57501

Tennessee
Office on Aging
Commission on Aging
9th Floor
Andrew Jackson Bldg.
500 Deaderick St.
Nashville, TN 37243

Medicaid Agency
Dep't. of Social Services
Medicaid Division
Citizen's Plaza Bldg.
12th Floor
400 Deaderick St.
Nashville, TN 37248-7350

Driver's License Authority
Dep't. of Safety
Driver Improvement Section
1150 Foster Ave.
Nashville, TN 37249

Texas
Office on Aging
Dep't. on Aging
PO Box 12786
Austin, TX 78711

Medicaid Agency
State Medicaid Director
Health and Human Services
  Commission
PO Box 13247
Austin, TX 78711

Driver's License Authority
Motor Vehicle Division
Dep't. of Transportation
Bldg. 150
200 East Riverside Drive
Austin, TX 78704

Utah
Office on Aging
Division of Aging & Adult
  Services
120 N. 200 W., Rm. 401
Salt Lake City, UT 84103

Medicaid Agency
Medicare/Medicaid Program
Certification & Resident
   Assessment
Health Dep't.
288 N. 1460 W.
Salt Lake City, UT 84116

Driver's License Authority
Dep't. of Public Safety
PO Box 30560
Salt Lake City, UT 84130-0560

Vermont
Office on Aging
Agency of Human Services
Dep't. of Aging & Disabilities
103 S. Main Street
Waterbury, VT 05671

Medicaid Agency
Medicaid Services Division
Dep't. of Social Welfare
103 S. Main St.
Waterbury, VT 05671-1201

Driver's License Authority
Agency of Transportation
Dep't. of Motor Vehicles
133 State St
Montpelier, VT 05602

Virginia
Office on Aging
Dep't. of Medical Assistance
   Services
Suite 102
Preston Bldg.
1600 Forest St.
Richmond, VA 23229

Medicaid Agency
Dep't. of Medical Assistance
   Services
Ste 1300
600 E. Broad Street
Richmond, VA 23219

Driver's License Authority
Dep't. of Motor Vehicles
2300 W. Broad Street
Richmond, VA 23220

Washington
Office on Aging
Aging & Adult Services Admin
Dep't. of Social & Health Services
PO Box 45050
Olympia, WA 98504

Medicaid Agency
Division of Medical Assistance
Dep't. of Social & Health Services
PO Box 45080
Olympia, WA 98504-5080

Driver's License Authority
Vehicle Services
Dep't. of Licensing
PO Box 48020
Olympia, WA 98507-8020

West Virginia
Office on Aging
Bureau of Senior Services
Holly Grove
1710 Kanawaha Blvd.
Charleston, WV 25311

Medicaid Agency
Dep't. of Health and Human
 Resources
Capitol Complex
Room 206, Bldg. 3
1900 Kanawha Blvd. East
Charleston, WV 25305

Driver's License Authority
Division of Motor Vehicles
Dep't. of Transportation
Room 337, Bldg. 3
1900 Kanawha Blvd. East
Charleston, WV 25305

Wisconsin
Office on Aging
Bureau on Aging
Dep't. of Health & Social Services
Suite 300
PO Box 7851
Madison, WI 53707

Medicaid Agency
Dep't. of Health & Family
 Services
PO Box 309
Madison, WI 53701-0309

Driver's License Authority
Division of Motor Vehicles
Dep't. of Transportation
PO Box 7949
Madison, WI 53707

Wyoming
Office on Aging
Division of Aging
Dep't. of Health
139 Hathaway Bldg.
2300 Capitol Ave
Cheyenne, WY 82002

Medicaid Agency
Health Care Financing
Dep't. of Health
6101 Yellowstone Road
Cheyenne, WY 82002

Driver's License Authority
Dep't. of Transportation
Driver License Control
5300 Bishop Blvd.
Box 1708
Cheyenne, WY 82002